CHILDREN'S DICTIONARY OF
OCCUPATIONS

Fourth Edition

By:

Barbara M. Parramore, Ed.D.
Professor Emeritus, Curriculum and Instruction
North Carolina State University
Raleigh, North Carolina

William E. Hopke, Ed.D.
Professor Emeritus, Counselor Education
North Carolina State University
Raleigh, North Carolina

with

Harry N. Drier, President
Career Education & Training Associates, Inc.
Educational Consultant
Singer Island, Florida

MERIDIAN EDUCATION CORPORATION
Lawrenceville, New Jersey

Fourth Edition

© 2004

By Meridian Education Corporation

2572 Brunswick Pike

Lawrenceville, New Jersey 08648

1-800-727-5507

Printed in U.S.A. Item No. 33584

ISBN: 07-365-9386-1

Cover Design and Illustrations by:

Ralston Scott Jones

dba artistudio, Normal, Illinois

scottjones@artistudio.org

Introduction

Students of all ages will work one day to earn a living. Work is part of living for grown-ups, just as going to school is part of a student's work. A school career includes kindergarten through grade twelve plus education or training beyond high school. Your work career will consist of the jobs or occupations that you do during your lifetime.

What Is This Book?

This book is a special kind of dictionary that lists job titles or occupations. Each job title has a definition or information about the occupation plus an illustration. Also, each of these occupations has been grouped into clusters to show you how jobs are related. In the Dictionary there are about 300 job titles about work that is done nearly every day somewhere in the United States. These job titles give you ideas about the many kinds of work that people do.

Why Have a Book Like This?

Is it too early to think about your future career? No, it's good to think and learn more about the kind of work you might like to do when you grow up. The more you think and plan for it, the happier you are likely to be when you do start to work.

People may change jobs several times in a lifetime, but often these jobs are related to each other. It's important to have work that you enjoy doing, because most people spend many hours every day at work.

What Kind of Jobs Are in the World of Work?

There are really three kinds. There's work to **make** things, like workers who make cars. Then there are people who work with **ideas and information**, like writers. Finally, there's work to **provide services,** like workers who deliver the mail. Some jobs or occupations require much knowledge and skill. Some kinds of work are easier to learn than others. Some people work outside in all kinds of weather while others work inside. Some workers wear uniforms and others do not. Some jobs require workers to use special tools or machines. Other jobs require thinking and planning. In the Dictionary you will learn about many different jobs.

What about the Future?

Selecting a career you like means finding work that is just right for you. Perhaps you like to meet and help people. Perhaps you like to work with numbers or designs. Perhaps you like to make things or help plants grow. Your particular talents and interests help you decide what may be best for your future career choice.

A career is more than a job. It is a choice about what is important to you and should include things that you like to do. Although most people are paid, it is not the only reason that people work. For example, volunteers are not paid for the work they do.

As you use the Dictionary, think about the choices of occupations you might make someday. Also, consider possible careers in your future. Jobs exist now that were not around ten years ago. Learn as much as you can about the tasks involved in different occupations. In any career it is important to read thoughtfully, write clearly, and use basic number facts. All of these skills are needed in nearly every occupation. Doing your best in the school world now will help you do your best in your future work.

A Note about Pronunciations

The phonetic pronunciations included in this dictionary are intended as a guide only. Since there are no official rules established regarding phonetic pronunciations, some experts may differ on the combinations of letters used to represent various sounds. Regional accents may also account for some differences. To help users pronounce the titles easily, words have been divided into syllables and all of the accents clearly shown.

The primary accent is printed in capital letters and bold type. /uh-**COUN**-tants/
A secondary accent is printed in capital letters without bold type. /in-**VES**-tih-GAY-ters/
Syllables that do not have an accent are typed in lower case letters. /child/care/WER-kers/

Budget Analysts

/BUD-jit/ /AN-uh-lists/

Companies must make money to stay in business. Budget analysts help businesses work efficiently without wasting money or other resources. They plan the costs and expenses of running an organization. They work in offices and often make use of computers and statistics. Budget analysts must be able to work with many other people in the workplace.

Using the Dictionary

The Dictionary can be used in a number of different ways. Have students look slowly through the job titles and drawings in the Children's Dictionary of Occupations. Or encourage students to look up specific job titles. They are listed in alphabetical order. Ask the following questions:

- Can you put yourself into any of the pictures?
- What are the workers doing?
- Can you imagine what the work is like?
- Turn to the back of the book to see the list of occupations in the index. Do any of the job titles interest you?

The Dictionary will also help students learn about jobs that are similar in some ways but not in others. For example, there are many different kinds of mechanics. One may repair a car, another an airplane, or another the diesel engine of a truck. This is also true for other occupations like clerks. Although nearly all clerks use computers to do work, the kind of work each clerk does is different.

Students using the Dictionary will learn more about occupations but they may also learn about words and their meanings. Notice that the names of some occupations have the same ending or suffix. For example, students may look for words that end in *ist*. This suffix means "a person who knows." A chemist is a person who knows chemistry. Students can look through the Dictionary to find as many occupations as they can that end in *ist*. Two other suffixes are often found at the end of occupational titles. These are *er* and *or*. They mean "a person who does," referring to the activity described in the first part of the word. A bricklayer is a person who lays bricks. A teacher is a person who teaches and a counselor is a person who counsels. Students may look for other occupational titles ending with either of these two suffixes. They will be practicing reading information with new words and terms. Using the Dictionary also helps students in using reference skills. Not only is there an alphabetical index of occupations with cross references, there are lists of jobs by occupational clusters.

How Many Job Choices Are Available?

There are more than 20,000 different occupations available in the United States. The titles chosen for the Dictionary were based on government information found in the 2002 - 2003 Occupational Outlook Handbook about the work force in the United States. Most of the job titles will be familiar and describe occupations that fit the majority of workers. However, some of the Dictionary titles will be new to students and may deserve further exploration.

Looking Ahead

The section called *Getting a Job* may be especially helpful for students. It provides information on finding a job, writing a résumé and cover letter, filling out a job application, and interviewing for a job. Although most students won't be seeking a job for several years, introducing them to the basic principles of employment will lay the groundwork for future career exploration.

Clusters of Related Occupations

The Occupational Outlook Handbook has grouped related occupations into clusters. This means that these jobs share common characteristics. If a job appeals to students in one category, they may be able to find other occupations in the same cluster that may be of interest.

Why Use a Cluster Approach?

1. It's impossible for individuals to research the thousands of occupations in the world of work. That would take a lot of time and effort.

2. Clusters help people understand how skills in a group of occupations are similar and may be transferable between occupations.

3. Students should focus on career fields, or groups of jobs, not individual occupations.

4. A cluster approach helps students understand concepts that apply to many occupations. These include interests, preparation for occupations, work settings, and special tools or equipment.

Every job title in this dictionary has been listed in a cluster area. The list begins on page 116.

Cluster Areas

Agriculture, Food & Natural Resources
Architecture & Construction
Arts, A/V Technology & Communications
Business, Management & Administration
Education & Training
Finance
Government & Public Administration
Health Science
Hospitality & Tourism
Human Services
Information Technology
Law, Public Safety & Security
Manufacturing
Marketing, Sales & Service
Science, Technology, Engineering & Mathematics
Transportation, Distribution & Logistics

Suggested Activities

Individual Activities

1. Look up names and pictures of job titles or occupations you already know about. Read the definitions to see if there's any new information.

2. Look in the back of the Dictionary to see the Alphabetical Index. See how many job titles are under the letters "D" and "J". Make a list of job titles that are of interest to you. Look up the definitions of the two most interesting. What did you learn?

3. Make a list of between five and eight jobs you know about. If you or your parents know someone who does one of these jobs, write his or her name beside the job title. Interview one of them and ask for information about his or her work. Find out where the work is done, what is done, and if any special tools or equipment are used. Ask the person if special training or education is needed to do the job.

4. In the Index, look for engineers under "E". You won't find a job title for engineer, yet there are many different kinds of engineers. Look under these letters to see the titles for different kinds of engineers: "A",

"C", "I", "M", and "N". How many are there? Can you write a definition for engineer? If not, explain why it is good to know what different kinds of engineers do in their work.

5. Recently, there are many more jobs for clerks. Skim through the Index to find at least three job titles with clerk. (There are more than 20.) Study the definitions of a few of these job titles. Where do the clerks do their work? What kind of work do they do? What knowledge or skills do they need? What are you learning in school that would be helpful if you were a clerk?

6. Conduct an interview about a job. Choose a family member, neighbor, or someone you know. Take notes, or you may wish to use a tape recorder. Ask the person to answer a few questions about the job. Think about the questions ahead of time. When the interview is over, thank the person for taking time to talk with you. Write a report about what you found out. You may wish to add or re-write the definition in the Dictionary.

Questions to Ask During a Job Interview

- What is the exact title of your job?
- What do you do on the job?
- Where do you work? (Outside, indoors, at a desk, on an assembly line.)
- Do you wear special clothes? What kind?
- Do you use special tools or equipment to do your job? What are they?
- When do you work? (Daytime, nights, weekends.)
- Do you need special knowledge to do your job?
- What do you like most about your work?

7. A career means all the jobs a person may have in a lifetime. Choose a senior citizen or a grandparent. Ask this person about the work he or she has done. If the person has had more than one job, write down the title of each main job. Ask the person how the jobs were alike and how they were different.

8. The "yellow pages" in the telephone book give information about workers and places of work in your community, town, or city. Find at least ten job titles in the "yellow

pages". For each one that is in the Dictionary, read the definitions and study the pictures. This will help you know more about your community and the kinds of work done there.

9. Look at the titles of the occupations and the illustrations as you skim through the Dictionary. Without reading the definitions, can you make a list of eight to ten occupations in which people have done work that has been helpful to you? Read the definitions. Compare what you already know with what you learned from reading the definitions. Look for others, too.

10. How many occupations can you find that tell about making things other than food, that you and your family need and use? List these on a separate sheet of paper. As you study and use the Dictionary, add occupations to your list. You may wish to review occupations in other groupings such as these:

- How many occupations can you find that tell about people who help keep us safe and healthy?

- How many occupations can you find that tell about people who work out-of-doors? At sea? On farms? In office buildings?

- How many occupations can you find that tell about people who work with heavy machinery? With their hands? At computers?

- How many occupations can you find that tell about people who build things?

- Which occupations require the person to use tools and special equipment to do the work?

- Which occupations require the person to travel?

- Which three or four occupations interest you enough to want to talk with a person in that job? Explain why you made that choice.

11. Advertisements often show persons at work. Look at ads on television or in magazines or newspapers. Choose one ad in which a person is working. Make a poster or a report about the ad and the worker. Show or explain how the worker helps the ad in getting its message across.

12. In this revised edition of the Dictionary, the authors found that computers have become even more important in the work that many people do. Become a detective and find at least five occupations in which a person uses computers to do work. Be a super sleuth and see how many more you can find.

Group Activities

1. Class Job Fair: Divide the group into two parts. Have each student choose three or four occupations in which they are interested. All of the occupations are listed and then each group decides on at least five occupations to look up in the Dictionary. They will discuss each job in a class meeting with the other group. Students may also plan posters, displays, and presentations to "sell" their occupations to other members of the group. On one day, half the class may serve as visitors to the Job Fair while the other half acts as potential employers. Roles are reversed on the second day.

2. Radio or Television Talk Show: Once students have selected and studied two or three occupations, the announcer interviews students one-at-a-time about an occupation. The announcer also allows others to "call in" with questions for the person who knows about the occupation. Look for evidence that the Dictionary entry has been studied.

3. Role Playing: Help students prepare or write a script for a television program on Available Jobs. The program will announce that people are needed to work at selected jobs. Each student will present one occupation. The point is to make the job so interesting that someone wants to do it. The announcer asks members of the audience how these occupations are alike or different. For example, some of these workers do things or provide services. Others make things. Some may work indoors while others work outside. Some may wear special clothing or use special tools. Ask students to decide if knowing how to read and write well or using mathematics may be important in some occupations. Some possible choices include: air traffic controllers, firefighters, graphic artists, hydrologists, industrial designers, jewelers, optometrists, roofers, sculptors, stock clerks, or others of interest in the local area.

4. Card Sorting: Print each title of the 16 clusters on cards or small squares of poster board. On smaller cards (or post-it notes) write the names of at least three occupations related to each cluster for a total of 48 small cards. Mix up the cards (or scatter the post-it notes on a bulletin board). Have students draw or select one or more cards then try to place each card in the correct cluster. As titles of occupations become more familiar, add cards to the set to make the activity more interesting and challenging.

5. Special Reports: Students may go to the library or school media center and locate books on occupations and jobs. Ask the librarian to assist in identifying books or stories about persons holding certain jobs. Sometimes a biography of a person includes information about the job or work the person did. Explore other resources of the media center for students interested in career planning and occupational information, including the electronic media such as CD-ROMs and the Internet. The counselor's office is another source of information.

Accountants and Auditors

/uh-COUN-tants/ and /AW-dih-ters/

Accountants and auditors work with numbers. They keep financial records for businesses, companies, the government, and individuals. These records show how much money is earned, how much is spent, and how much is paid for taxes. To audit means to check for mistakes and to correct them. Accountants and auditors must be neat and careful in their work. They are good at solving math problems and working with computers.

Actuaries

/AC-tu-air-ees/

Actuaries gather information to help insurance companies and other businesses make decisions about insurance policies and other financial plans. Companies and people pay for insurance so that, when loss and accidents happen, they can file a "claim" and receive money from the insurance company to get them back on their feet. Actuaries use math formulas to figure out how much money a company may have to pay in claims. They make sure that insurance companies charge enough for the policies so that there is plenty of money to pay for all the claims. Actuaries must be good in math to do this work.

Adjusters and Investigators

/uh-JUS-ters/ and /in-VES-tih-GAY-ters/

Adjusters, investigators, and collectors work for insurance companies, department stores, banks, and government agencies. When people file claims for money to pay for a loss or damage, investigators and adjusters make sure the claims are real and should be paid. Then they decide how much money the person who filed the claim should receive.

Administrative Services Managers

/ad-MIN-iss-TRAY-tiv/ /SER-vis-es/
/MAN-uh-jers/

These managers work in both private industry and government jobs. They supervise employees who provide supportive services for a company or office, such as typing letters and driving delivery trucks. They may also manage other departments such as mail, library, printing, or other activities needed to run large firms or offices.

Adult and Vocational Education Teachers

/uh-DULT/ and /vo-KAY-shuh-nul/ /ed-u-KAY-shun/ /TEE-chers/

Just like young people, grown-ups like to learn about new and interesting subjects. Sometimes, they also need to learn new working skills to use in their jobs or to change careers. Teaching adults is the job of adult and vocational education teachers. They teach classes in factories and office buildings, museums, hospitals, community colleges, and other locations. They often teach in the evenings and on weekends when working people can attend classes.

Aerospace Engineers

/AIR-o-space/ /EN-ji-NEERS/

Aerospace engineers plan, build, and test all kinds of spacecraft and aircraft. They work on rockets, missiles, and satellites as well as airplanes and helicopters. They work for the military and for companies that make equipment and parts for these machines. Like all engineers, aerospace engineers should be able to work as members of a team, to solve problems, and to think of new ideas.

Agricultural Scientists and Agronomists

/ag-rih-**KUL**-chur-ul/
/**SY**-en-tists/
and /uh-
GRON-uh-
mists/

All agricultural
scientists study ways
to produce farm crops
and animals more
efficiently. They
share ideas with farmers and with
companies that make fertilizer, seeds, and
food. There are different kinds of scientists
interested in growing agricultural products.
Some study only certain kinds of animals,
such as cows or chickens. Others study soil
or fruits or plant diseases. Agronomists
have a special interest in farm crops such
as corn, wheat, cotton, and soybeans. They
work to help farmers grow healthier plants
and to harvest more crops from their land.
Agricultural scientists and agronomists
work in laboratories and outdoors.

Air Traffic Controllers

/air/ /**TRAF**-fic/
/kon-**TROL**-lers/

Air traffic controllers work in the control
tower at airports. They direct planes that
are in the air and on the runways. They
give directions and advice to pilots over a
two-way radio. They tell pilots when it is
safe to take off or to land planes and how
low or high to fly them. They also make
sure that planes are flying safe distances
apart. They must be able to make
decisions quickly and to speak clearly.
The Federal Aviation Administration
trains and hires air traffic controllers.

Aircraft Mechanics and Engine Specialists

/**AIR**-craft/ /muh-**KAN**-iks/
and /**EN**-jin/ /**SPEH**-shul-ists/

Aircraft mechanics and engine specialists keep planes and helicopters
in good working condition. Before every flight, they inspect the engines,
landing gear, and instruments. They make any needed repairs, replace
worn parts, and check for rust and cracks in the metal. Aircraft mechanics
usually work in hangars at airports or for companies that build planes.

Aircraft Pilots

/AIR-craft/ /PIE-luhts/

On large aircraft, three pilots are needed on flights. Aircraft pilots and copilots fly planes that carry passengers and cargo. They check maps, flight plans, and weather reports. The pilot, called a captain by the airlines, is in charge of all the crew members on a plane. Co-pilots help steer the plane and study the dials on the cockpit panel. They talk to air traffic controllers on a two-way radio. Anyone who flies a plane must have a pilot's license from the Federal Aviation Administration.

Amusement and Recreation Attendants

/uh-**MUSE**-ment/ and /**REK**-ree-**AY**-shun/ /uh-**TEN**-dants/

Amusement and recreation attendants perform various jobs at parks, sports facilities, and amusement parks. They might be hired by a city park system to collect money and assign locker space at a swimming pool or to maintain equipment in a gymnastics club or a gymnasium. They assist rangers at national parks by checking campsites and painting picnic shelters. Other duties may include scheduling use of facilities, setting bowling pins, preparing billiard tables, and operating carnival rides and amusement concessions.

Anthropologists

/an-thro-**POL**-uh-jists/

Anthropologists are social scientists who study what groups of people believe and how they live, work, and play together. They look at the ways in which people talk to each other and treat each other, the clothes they wear, and the food they eat. Some anthropologists are interested in people who live in all parts of the world today. Others try to discover more about people who lived long ago. Physical anthropologists study skeletons to discover what the earliest people on earth looked like. Most anthropologists work for colleges and museums.

Antique Dealers

/an-TEEK/ /DEAL-ers/

Antique dealers buy and sell furniture, toys, clothing, and all sorts of things that were made long ago. They're like treasure hunters, always looking for a chair or a toy drum that's very old and valuable. Usually they work in their own store, where they sell what they've found, and even buy antiques to resell. They may even make trips across America and to other countries to find things to bring back and sell.

Apparel Workers

/uh-PAIR-el/ /WER-kers/

Apparel means clothing. Apparel workers work for textile and knit goods industries, where the clothes we wear are designed, made, and sold. There are many steps in the manufacturing process, so there are many different jobs for apparel workers. Some workers operate cutting, sewing, or knitting machines or computers. Others inspect the finished product for quality and size. Some prepare the garments for shipping.

Archaeologists

/ar-kee-OL-uh-jists/

Archaeologists are curious about the daily life of people who lived long ago. They look for clues by digging up buried cities and villages and by exploring caves and tombs. They find things like jewelry, tools, weapons, and pottery. These artifacts are like pieces of a puzzle that can be put together to get a better picture of what happened in the past. The work of archaeologists helps us understand the history of people all over the world.

Architects

/AR-kih-TECS/

Architects design homes, office buildings, churches, museums, and even parks and airports. They need to know the building's purpose to help them plan how the building will look. They must also think about how to make it a safe place for the people who will use it. Architects draw very detailed plans called blueprints that are instructions for the builders to follow. Architects also decide if a building will be made of steel, glass, bricks, or other materials.

Archivists and Curators

/AR-kih-vists/ and /KURE-ate-ers/

People who work in museums know how to identify, organize, preserve, and display things that should be saved for future generations. Curators are in charge of collections of objects such as old tools, weapons, furniture, or paintings. Archivists work with letters, manuscripts, battle plans, and other documents. If you are interested in history and curious about how things change over time, these careers are good choices for you.

Armed Forces Occupations

/armed/ /FOR-ces/ /OC-u-PAY-shuns/

The armed forces are the different parts of the United States Military and are responsible for protecting the United States. These include the Army, Navy, Air Force, Marine Corps, and Coast Guard. Soldiers, sailors, and other people in the armed forces do many types of jobs. Some jobs are in offices, hospitals, and schools. Others are on ships or airplanes. When people join the military, they are given tests to find out which jobs are best for them. Then they go to special schools and receive training to do the job.

Artists

/AR-tists/

Artists create and perform in ways that require special talent or skill. Their work is recognized by other people as interesting, entertaining, or pleasing to the senses. There are different areas of art, such as painting, music, dancing, or sculpture. In each area, people who study, practice, and work to develop their skills are called artists. A musician who plays an instrument very well and one who composes new tunes are both artists.

Astronomers

/uh-**STRON**-uh-mers/

Astronomers study the universe and its stars, galaxies, and planets. They chart the paths of comets and asteroids. The size of the planet Earth, its shape, its age, and the air around it are also of interest to astronomers. These scientists use mathematics and physics to tell about their discoveries. Astronomers also use tools such as telescopes, spectrometers, and computers.

Astrophysicists

/AS-tro-**FIZZ**-ih-cists/

Astrophysicists are both physicists and astronomers. They connect what they know about matter and energy to the study of the universe. They use their knowledge of heat, light, magnetism, and motion to answer questions about the sun or planets. Astrophysicists use tools such as a laser range-finder to measure the distance between the earth and the moon.

Athletes

/ATH-letes/

Athletes participate in sports. When they are paid to play, they are called professional athletes. In some sports, athletes are members of a team. They have a certain job to do to help the team win. Football, basketball, baseball, and soccer are team sports. Some athletes compete with another player one-to-one. Others, like tennis players, golfers, and wrestlers, are paid prize money when they win in tournaments. Athletes spend many hours practicing. They also travel a lot.

Automotive Body Repairers

/AW-tuh-MO-tiv/
/BAH-dee/ /re-PAIR-ers/

Automotive body repairers remove dents, straighten crumpled fenders, and replace ruined parts of cars and trucks. They use metal-cutting guns, torches, and welding equipment. When they repair vehicles, they try to make them look smooth and return them to their original shape. Automotive body repairers also replace broken glass in car windows and lights. They must know a lot about how cars and trucks are built and what materials are used in different parts.

Automotive Mechanics

/AW-tuh-MO-tiv/
/muh-KAN-iks/

Mechanics who repair cars and trucks are called automotive mechanics. They work on the engines and adjust brakes. They clean radiators and spark plugs and replace broken parts in engines. Automotive mechanics must be good at figuring out exactly what the problem is when a vehicle breaks down or does not run well. Most automotive mechanics work at auto repair shops and car dealerships.

Automotive Refinishers

/AW-tuh-**MO**-tiv/
/ree-**FIN**-ish-ers/

Before automotive refinishers can begin to paint a car, truck, or motorcycle, they and their helpers use power sanders and sandpaper to remove all the old paint and rust. Then they fill in any dents in the car's surface. They use a spray gun to apply several coats of paint. If they're only painting part of a car, they may have to mix paints to match the old paint color, which may have faded.

Baggage Porters and Bellhops

/**BAG**-ij/ /**POR**-ters/
and /**BELL**-hops/

Baggage porters and bellhops help people at air, bus, and train stations and those who are staying in a hotel or motel. They carry heavy suitcases and help the guests find their rooms. They also give people directions and assist handicapped persons.

Bank Branch Managers

/bank/ /branch/ /**MAN**-uh-jers/

Bank branch managers are in charge of a special kind of business. Banks offer many different kinds of money services to people. Some of these are savings and checking accounts. People may get loans to build a house or to buy a car from a bank. Bank managers give advice about saving money and how to invest it. Making an investment is a way of buying something now that may be worth more money in the future. Bank managers are in charge of other workers in a bank.

Bank Tellers

/bank/ /TELL-ers/

Bank tellers work behind the counter in a bank. They help people put their money in or take it out of their bank accounts. Bank tellers count money very, very carefully. They keep records of the amounts of money deposited and withdrawn from accounts. They also cash checks, file checks and records, and count large sums of money. Bank tellers must be helpful and friendly to a bank's customers.

Barbers

/BAR-bers/

Barbers shampoo, cut, trim, and style hair. They can dye or bleach hair to another color. They give permanents to make hair curly or straight. Barbers also trim beards and mustaches, give shaves, and help people who wear wigs choose the right style and color. Barbers work with scissors, clippers, razors, and dryers. They clean and sweep their work areas. Barbers who own or manage a shop must order supplies, pay bills, and hire other barbers to work in the barbershop. They must be able to get along well with their customers.

Bicycle Repairers

/BY-SIK-uhl/ /re-PAIR-ers/

Bicycle repairers fix broken bikes. There are many kinds to repair, such as road bikes, speed racing bikes, and mountain bikes. Repairers must be able to find the problem and then fix it. They use different hand tools, like pliers, wrenches, and screwdrivers. These workers need to listen carefully to what a customer says. Most repairers learn by experience.

Billing Clerks

/**BILL**-ing/ /clerks/

Billing clerks keep records of the amounts of money a business earns and spends. They send out bills to customers, receive payments, and enter the amounts in ledger books or in computers. They use calculators and computers in their work. Billing clerks are employed in many places. These include government offices, hospitals, department stores, credit card companies, and all businesses.

Bindery Workers

/**BIND**-er-ee/ /**WER**-kers/

Books, catalogs, calendars, and other printed materials are put together in a bindery. The pages are gathered, organized, and sewn or glued together by bindery workers. These workers operate machines that stack, trim, paste, and press. They check to make sure the pictures and pages are in the correct order. Some bindery workers restore old or damaged books and design special covers.

Biochemists

/**BY**-o-**KEM**-ists/

Biochemists study the chemicals that are combined in all living things. They examine cells to learn more about how plants and animals grow and reproduce. By understanding the materials that are in living matter, biochemists help people live healthier lives and farmers grow better crops. Biochemists also develop and test new medicines. They work in laboratories where they do experiments with chemicals. Many of them teach at universities.

Biological Scientists, Botanists, and Zoologists

/BY-o-**LOJ**-ih-kul/ /**SY**-en-tists/ /**BOT**-uh-nists/ and /zoe-**OL**-uh-jists/

Biological scientists study plant and animal life. In science, the word for life is "bio". Biological scientists are interested in all living things. They wonder about the ways living things are the same or are different. Some biological scientists study forms of life that can only be seen through a microscope. Others, known as zoologists, study animals like birds or fish or mammals. Botanists study plants and how they grow. They are interested in the different parts of plants such as the stem, roots, leaves, and seeds. All biological scientists search for answers about how things grow and reproduce, and the best environment for life.

Blue-Collar Worker Supervisors

/blue/ /**COL**-ler/ /**WER**-ker/ /**SUE**-purr-**VY**-zers/

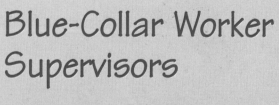

Blue-collar worker supervisors direct workers and teams of workers. They are responsible for seeing that a job is done well and completed on time. They make sure that people show up for work, that new workers are trained, and that everyone is using materials and equipment correctly. Blue-collar supervisors are also called foremen, forewomen, or crew bosses. They are in charge of workers in factories and mines, workers who are building roads or houses, and workers who load trucks and ships.

Bookkeeping, Accounting, and Auditing Clerks

/**BOOK**-KEEP-ing/ /uh-**COUNT**-ing/ and /**AW**-dih-ting/ /clerks/

Bookkeeping, accounting, and auditing clerks keep accurate and careful records. They show how money was earned and spent by businesses. They take orders from customers. Then they prepare copies of the customer's bill which shows how much money is owed. After bills are mailed, bookkeeping, accounting, and auditing clerks keep records of who has paid and who has not. They also write paychecks for workers and keep files about taxes. These workers use calculators and computers to do their work. They may also do some general office work such as filing and answering the telephone.

Bricklayers and Stonemasons

/BRICK-LAY-ers/ and /STONE-MAY-sons/

Bricklayers and stonemasons use bricks, concrete blocks, and stones to build houses and other buildings, fireplaces, walls, and walkways. Bricklayers mix mortar to hold the bricks together. Stonemasons use chisels and hammers to cut big blocks of marble and granite. Some of them also make tombstones. Bricklayers and stonemasons learn their skills by serving as apprentices, or helpers, for experienced workers.

Broadcast Technicians

/BROAD-cast/ /tek-NISH-uns/

Broadcast technicians operate the electrical equipment used to produce radio and television shows. They work in television or radio studios with video and audio recorders, microphones, and lights. Television cameras are run by broadcast technicians. So is the equipment used to make CDs, news programs, music videos, and commercials.

Budget Analysts

/BUD-jit/ /AN-uh-lists/

Companies must make money to stay in business. Budget analysts help businesses work efficiently without wasting money or other resources. They plan the costs and expenses of running an organization. They work in offices and often make use of computers and statistics. Budget analysts must be able to work with many other people in the workplace.

Bus Drivers

/bus/ /DRY-vers/

Bus drivers drive buses that travel within a city as well as buses that travel long distances. They collect fares, take tickets, and give information to their passengers. Bus drivers are also responsible for passenger safety. They drive carefully and make sure that fire extinguishers, first-aid kits, and emergency reflectors are always on the bus. Bus drivers must be able to get along well with all kinds of people.

Butchers and Meat, Poultry, and Fish Cutters

/BUTCH-ers/ and /meat/ /POLE-tree/ and /fish/ /CUT-ters/

Butchers and meat, poultry, and fish cutters cut large pieces of these products into smaller pieces for people to buy. They prepare beef, pork, poultry, fish, and other meats so that they are ready to cook. Butchers work in grocery stores, restaurants, and meat packing plants. Their work is usually done in very cold places so the meat doesn't spoil.

Buyers, Wholesale and Retail

/BY-ers/ /HOLE-SALE/ and /REE-tail/

Buyers in retail and wholesale trade are the "go-betweens" for companies that make things and stores that sell things to customers. Buyers must keep up with what customers will want to buy and what new products are on the market. They help stores look for the best quality and the best price. Sometimes they handle orders for many different stores, but some buyers work for just one store. Some travel all over the world to find things for a store to sell.

Camp Counselors

/camp/ /COUN-seh-lers/

Camp counselors supervise the activities of children at recreational camps. Some teach crafts, such as weaving or painting. Others teach sports, such as swimming or archery. Some lead nature hikes, singing, or games. Camp counselors are responsible for the safety of campers. Some have duties in maintaining camp facilities and equipment.

Carpenters

/CAR-pen-ters/

Carpenters build houses, office buildings, cabinets, decks, and other things made of wood. Using power tools, they cut and shape wood and other building materials. They use hammers, saws, chisels, planes, and drills. Carpenters must follow blueprints and make careful measurements. Most carpenters work in teams. Others are in business for themselves and are hired to remodel houses, add new rooms, or build bookshelves, garages, or even doghouses.

Carpet Installers

/CAR-pet/ /in-STALL-ers/

Carpet installers work in homes and other buildings. They put carpet and carpet pads on floors. First, they prepare the wood, concrete, or metal floors and make careful measurements. Then they cut, match, and fit the carpet using tape, glue, tacks, and nails. Workers who install floor coverings must do a lot of bending, kneeling, stretching, and lifting. They use handtools such as carpet knives and power stretchers.

Cashiers

/ka-SHEERS/

Cashiers operate cash registers in department stores, clothing stores, supermarkets, and fast-food restaurants. They collect money from customers, give change, and count money at the end of the business day. They often do double-duty as sales clerks and cashiers. Some cashiers are called checkout clerks. In movie theaters, cashiers sell tickets.

Chefs, Cooks, and Food Preparation Workers

/shefs/ /cooks/ and /food/ /PREP-er-RAY-shun/ /WER-kers/

Cooks and chefs prepare food in restaurants, hospitals, schools, and other places. A chef is a cook who has more training, skill, or experience. Many chefs are famous for creating new recipes and writing cookbooks. In large kitchens, each cook has a special assignment, like being in charge of meat, vegetables, sauces, or salads. Cooks and chefs must please their customers with food that tastes good and also looks good. Other kitchen workers help prepare food and clean work areas and utensils.

Chemical Engineers

/KEM-ih-kul/ /EN-ji-NEERS/

Chemical engineers use their knowledge of chemistry, physics, and mathematics to make chemical products. Plastic, rubber, pesticides, and paper are a few of the many things made with chemicals. Some chemical engineers help design and build factories and laboratories or containers for storing chemicals. They design machinery used to mix chemicals and create ways to make new materials.

Chemists

/KEM-ists/

Chemists work in laboratories where they mix and test chemicals. They keep records and write reports about the results of their experiments. Their research may lead to new chemical products such as drugs to cure diseases. Some chemists specialize in medical research. Some work for chemical industries. Chemists also study the earth's environment and work to reduce pollution in our air and water.

Child Care Workers

/child/ /care/ /WER-kers/

Child care workers are teachers and helpers in daycare centers or nursery schools. They help take care of young children while parents are working at jobs. They plan things for the children to do such as games, art projects, story hour, and play periods. They teach children about safety, healthy foods, numbers, letters, and colors. Sometimes they take children on field trips in the community. Child care workers are interested in helping children learn to get along with others.

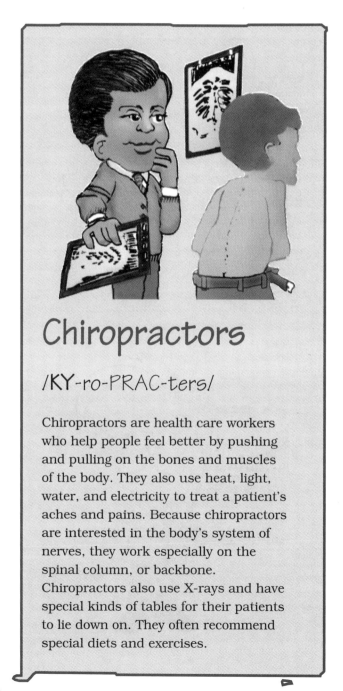

Chiropractors

/KY-ro-PRAC-ters/

Chiropractors are health care workers who help people feel better by pushing and pulling on the bones and muscles of the body. They also use heat, light, water, and electricity to treat a patient's aches and pains. Because chiropractors are interested in the body's system of nerves, they work especially on the spinal column, or backbone. Chiropractors also use X-rays and have special kinds of tables for their patients to lie down on. They often recommend special diets and exercises.

Civil Engineering Technicians

/SIV-ul/ /EN-ji-NEER-ing/ /tek-NISH-uns/

Civil engineering technicians work closely with civil engineers to plan and build highways, public buildings, power plants, and bridges. The technicians help draw the plans and check to see that projects are built correctly. Some are responsible for maintenance and repairs so that these places will be safe for people to use. Civil engineering technicians also test materials like the concrete and steel used in building roads, buildings, or dams.

Civil Engineers

/SIV-ul/ /EN-ji-NEERS/

Civil engineers design and plan roads, tunnels, bridges, dams, and airports. They direct the construction workers who build these large projects. Civil engineers also help plan cities and the water and waste systems used by all the people who live in cities. They work for the government or for construction firms. Many civil engineers are hired by utility companies that supply electric power or telephone services and light.

Clerical Supervisors and Managers

/CLAIR-ih-kul/
/SUE-purr-VY-zers/
and /MAN-uh-jers/

Clerical work includes such tasks as word processing, filing, photocopying, and answering telephones. Hiring, training, planning, and evaluating the work of a clerical staff is the job of supervisors or managers. They must know what work needs to be done in a business office and must make certain the work is done well and on time.

Clinical Laboratory Technologists and Technicians

/CLIN-ih-kul/ /LAB-rah-TOR-ee/ /tek-NOL-uh-jists/ and /tek-NISH-uns/

Clinical laboratory personnel perform tests to help find out what's wrong when someone is sick. They work in hospitals and health clinics examining samples of blood, urine, and other body fluids and tissues. Workers use microscopes to look for changes in human cells which show the presence of diseases. Doctors use the laboratory test results to decide how to treat the patient.

Coaches and Sports Instructors

/KO-ches/ and /sports/ /in-STRUK-ters/

Coaches and sports instructors help both students and professional athletes who play individual and team sports. Coaches train athletes for competition by holding practice sessions to improve the athletes' performance and conditioning. Coaches also manage the team during practice sessions and competitions by making sure they have what they need to compete and win. They direct team strategy, call plays, look for new players, and teach good sportsmanship and fairness. Sports instructors usually teach individual athletes who compete in sports like bowling, golf, swimming, gymnastics, and tennis. They decide what kinds of exercises the athlete should do to improve his or her performance, and help the athlete be the best at a chosen sport.

College and University Faculty Members

/CAH-lij/ and /U-nih-VER-sih-tee/ /FAC-ul-tee/ /MEM-bers/

College and university faculty are teachers who work with college students. They are also called professors. College professors must study for many years to learn about the subjects they teach. Their work is learning and teaching. They may conduct experiments to learn new things. They write books and articles. Sometimes they speak at conferences to share their ideas and discoveries. They work in offices, classrooms, libraries, and laboratories.

Commercial and Industrial Electronics Equipment Repairers

/cuh-**MER**-shul/ and /in-**DUS**-tree-ul/ /ee-lek-**TRON**-iks/ /ee-**KWIP**-ment/ /re-**PAIR**-ers/

Commercial and industrial electronics equipment repairers work with equipment that makes or is powered by electricity. They help engineers plan and make new equipment and products such as appliances, computers, robots, and satellites. They also install and repair electrical systems for factories, power companies, and telephone companies. Technicians know a lot about tubes, transistors, wires, microchips, and other electrical parts. They work with tools, from a simple screwdriver to complex measuring devices.

Communications Equipment Mechanics

/cuh-**MU**-nih-**KAY**-shuns/ /ee-**KWIP**-ment/ /muh-**KAN**-iks/

These mechanics work on the equipment used in phone systems, cable and satellite television systems, and the Internet. They use tools such as screwdrivers and soldering (sod-der-ing) guns to connect wires and cables. They test the flow of electricity through the wires with special machines.

Computer Animators

/com-**PEW**-ter/ /**AN**-im-may-ters/

These artists work on computers to create the television cartoons and animated movies we see in theaters, as well as in commercials and computer games. They create "special effects" like making it look like a hero is flying or being chased by a monster. You have to know a lot about the computer to be a computer animator. You have to be a good artist too!

Computer Programmers

/com-**PEW**-ter/ /**PRO**-gram-mers/

Computer programmers write the step-by-step instructions that tell computers how to organize information and solve problems. These programs are written in a special language or code which the computer can read. Programmers also write instruction sheets for the computer operators who run the programs.

Computer Software Engineers

/com-**PEW**-ter/ /**SOFT**-ware/ /EN-ji-**NEERS**/

Someone has to tell a computer what to do, and that's the job of a computer software engineer. They instruct a computer by writing line after line of computer "code". Sometimes they fix a computer program that isn't working the way it should, and other times they create new programs to make a computer do things that computers have never done before. Computer software engineers know a lot about computers, and they know a lot about math too. And they never know when a new problem is going to come up that they'll have to fix.

Computer Support Specialists

/com-**PEW**-ter/ /sup-**PORT**/ /**SPEH**-shul-ists/

Many people who use computers don't really understand how their computer works, so they might run into problems they can't fix on their own. That's where a computer support specialist comes in. Whether they work for the store where you buy a computer, or for the company that makes them, their job is to answer questions and help solve problems for the people who use the computers. And if they get a lot of questions about one problem, they can tell the company that the problem should be corrected. So you could say they help make tomorrow's computers even better!

Computer Systems Analysts

/com-**PEW**-ter/ /**SIS**-tems/ /**AN**-uh-lists/

Computer systems analysts design and plan ways in which computers can do work for businesses, banks, scientists, engineers, or writers. They understand just what computers are able to do. Then they match the work that needs to be done with the right kind of computer equipment and the right programs. They work with programmers to write the instructions that will run the computers. Systems analysts also draw charts and diagrams to help explain things to computer operators.

Concrete Masons and Terrazzo Workers

/**CON**-creet/ /**MAY**-sons/ and /teh-**ROT**-so/ /**WER**-kers/

Concrete masons and terrazzo workers build things with materials made of crushed rocks and stones. Cement, also called concrete, is used for small jobs such as sidewalks and patios. It is also used for big jobs like superhighways and dams. Terrazzo is a tile used for floors, stairs, and decorations in buildings. Cement masons and terrazzo workers must mix, pour, mold, and create a smooth and level surface. They use wheelbarrows, trowels, hoes, and levels in their work.

Construction and Building Inspectors

/con-**STRUK**-shun/ and /**BIL**-ding/ /in-**SPEC**-ters/

Construction and building inspectors work for federal, state, and local governments. They are responsible for checking on the safety of roads, sewer and water systems, bridges, and buildings. Builders must follow rules or "code regulations" that guarantee the quality of their work. Construction and building inspectors check to be sure the code regulations are followed. They test the strength of concrete, look at wiring and plumbing, study blueprints, and write reports. They can stop the work on a project until all mistakes have been corrected.

Construction Machinery Operators

/con-**STRUK**-shun/
/muh-**SHEEN**-er-ree/
/**OP**-er-**ATE**-ers/

Construction machinery operators run the big equipment used at building sites and to build highways. Skill and strength are needed to operate bulldozers, jackhammers, cranes, dump trucks, or paving machines. Other construction machinery includes derricks, pile drivers, and concrete mixers. Operators must also know how to do repairs. Their work is noisy and is out of doors during all kinds of weather.

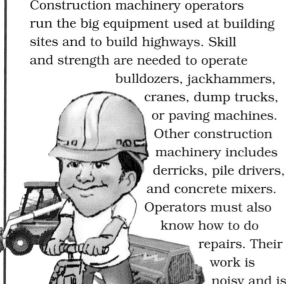

Copy Writers

/**COP**-ee/ /**RYE**-ters/

Copy writers write advertisements. These ads are used in newspapers and magazines and on radio and television. The purpose of an advertisement is to sell a product or business service. Copy writers must choose words, phrases, and images that get attention. They must give facts about the product or service. Some copy writers write the brochures or instructions that come with a product.

Correctional Officers

/cor-**REK**-shun-ul/ /**OFF**-ih-sirs/

Correctional officers are in charge of people who are serving sentences in jails or prisons. They keep order within these places and enforce rules and regulations. Correctional officers must keep a close watch on everything the inmates do. Some serve as guards on towers or at the gates. Counseling and helping inmates with problems are also important duties of a correctional officer.

Cosmetologists

/COS-meh-**TOL**-uh-jists/

Cosmetologists wash, cut, and style people's hair. They also lighten or darken the color of hair and clean and style wigs. They may help their customers take care of their skin, fingernails, and toenails. Cosmetologists are also called hairstylists and beauticians. Those who own or manage a shop keep records, order supplies, and hire other cosmetologists to work in the shop. Related workers include manicurists, artists who apply makeup, and electrologists who remove hair from skin by electrolysis.

Cost Estimators

/cost/ /**ES**-teh-**MAY**-ters/

People in charge of making things need to know in advance what the total cost will be. Plans may be to build something, manufacture a product, or improve a way of making or doing things. Cost estimators gather information on all the expenses involved. The estimates may be for workers, equipment, materials, transporting what is needed to the work site, even housing and feeding workers when necessary. Using their careful judgment, they put together an estimated, or approximate, cost which is used to determine whether the project is affordable.

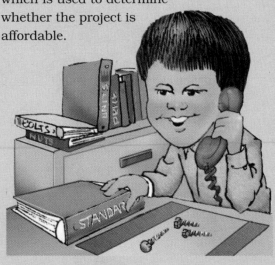

Counselors

/**COUN**-seh-lers/

Counselors help people learn to understand themselves better. They help them solve their problems and make important choices about their lives. Sometimes, counselors give advice, but their most important job is to listen carefully to the people who talk to them. School counselors help students learn study skills. They help them learn about careers and how to get along with their friends, teachers, or families. Some counselors work with people who have disabilities or with prisoners.

Counter and Rental Clerks

/COUN-ter/ and /RENT-ul /clerks/

Most stores and shops have a counter or checkout area where customers pay for their purchases or for services they have received. Clerks add up the total cost, take the customer's money, give change and receipts, and package the items. These workers also answer questions for customers, and may stock the shelves and do other tasks in the store.

Court Reporters

/cort/ /ree-POR-ters/

Court reporters make written reports of statements, meetings, court cases, and other events that need legal records. They listen carefully and use a special machine to write down everything that is said. They must record every word exactly and cannot add anything or leave anything out. Every court case uses a court reporter but most work outside of the courtroom. Reporters work with lawyers, state and local governments, and other agencies.

Credit Clerks and Authorizers

/CRED-it/ /clerks/ and /AW-tho-RYE-zers/

Credit clerks and authorizers work in offices. When someone applies for a loan, credit clerks gather all of the necessary information and make sure the loan application is filled out completely. They keep up with a person's credit rating. Your credit rating tells people whether you pay your bills on time, so they can decide if they want to lend you money. Authorizers use credit ratings in doing their work. They use it to decide whether a person may buy something on credit and pay later. This information is given to businesses or stores who ask for it. Authorizers and credit clerks use computers and telephones in doing their work.

Credit Counselors

/CRED-it/ /COUN-seh-lers/

Sometimes people buy too many things "on credit"—using credit cards and loans—and then realize that they don't have enough money to pay for what they bought. So they ask a credit counselor for help. Credit counselors help them figure out how they can pay back the money they owe, and how much they can afford to buy in the future. Credit counselors sometimes call the people the money is owed to and ask them if the money can be paid back in small amounts, so that it's easier to pay. They usually work for companies that just help people with money problems, but sometimes they work with banks or other companies too.

Customer Service Representatives

/CUS-tuh-mer/ /SER-vis/
/REP-pree-ZEN-tuh-tivs/

People in these jobs help solve problems. They listen to customer problems and find a way to help. Customers may call, write letters, or visit the company. These workers need to be patient and not get angry when customers get upset. They need to know all about company products and be able to answer questions. They must also keep good and accurate records.

Cytotechnologists

/SY-toe-tek-NOL-uh-jists/

Cytotechnologists are special kinds of clinical workers. They examine human body cells through a microscope. They look for signs of disease. Some diseases, like cancer, change the size and shape of cells. Cytotechnologists know how to recognize these changes. Their reports help doctors decide what to do for the patient. Cytotechnologists work in hospitals, laboratories, and places where cancer research is done.

Dancers and Choreographers

/DANS-ers/ and
/cor-ree-OG-ruh-fers/

Dancers are entertainers whose special body movements require skill and training. Since most dances are performed to music, dancers need a sense of rhythm. They often dance with a team but sometimes perform alone. Most dancers practice very hard to become artists in a special area of dancing, such as ballet, tap, or jazz. Dancers who create new dance routines for others to perform are called choreographers.

Dental Assistants

/DEN-tul/ /uh-SIS-tents/

Dental assistants work with dentists as they examine and treat a person's teeth or gums. They make patients comfortable in the chair, get their dental records or charts, and take care of the tools and equipment used by dentists. Dental assistants take X-rays and mix materials for fillings. Some dental assistants also do office work such as making appointments and sending bills.

Dental Hygienists

/DEN-tul / /hy-JEN-ists/

Dental hygienists are trained to clean people's teeth and to teach people how to keep their teeth and gums healthy and clean. They also help dentists by checking a patient's teeth for signs of decay and by taking X-rays. Some dental hygienists work in schools where they check children's teeth. They also show students how to brush and floss properly, and they teach them about eating foods that help build strong teeth.

Dental Laboratory Technicians

/DEN-tul / /LAB-rah-TOR-ee/ /tek-NISH-uns/

Dental laboratory technicians make false teeth, crowns, bridges, and braces. These and other things are used by dentists to repair teeth. The technicians use metal, plastic, and porcelain to make these items. They make molds of wax or plaster. They use carving tools, drills, and metal-melting torches. Dental laboratory technicians must be very good at working with their hands and at making small, detailed things well.

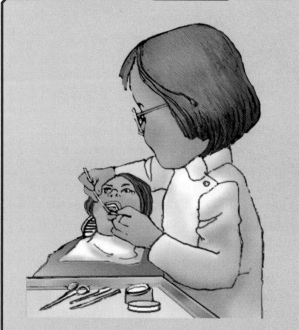

Dentists

/DEN-tists/

Dentists are doctors specially trained to take care of people's teeth and gums. They look for decay or diseases by examining the mouth and by studying X-rays. They fill cavities, repair broken teeth, straighten teeth, and treat diseases of the gums. Dentists remove teeth that are too full of decay to be saved. They replace them with false teeth. Sometimes dentists also perform surgery on the gums or jawbone.

Designers

/dee-ZINE-ers/

Designers work to make the places and things we use pleasing to look at. Pleasant surroundings or beautiful clothes and flowers can boost our spirits. Products in interesting packages catch our attention and make us want to buy them. Designers know about color, shapes, textures, and materials. There are fashion designers, floral designers, and designers who decorate and furnish homes and offices. Set designers create the scenery and settings for stage shows and movies. Architects, urban planners, graphic artists, and people who design cars, furniture, or toys are also designers. All are interested in the ways things look.

Desktop Publishers and Typesetters

/DESK-top/ /PUB-lish-ers/ and /TYPE-SET-ers/

Desktop publishers and typesetters operate machines that print words on books, magazines, newspapers, and posters. On older printing presses, the letters were cut out of wood or metal. Now, most typesetting is done with computers. The desktop publishers and typesetters must work quickly but carefully. They must check spelling and arrange words and pictures on a page.

Diesel Mechanics

/DEE-zul/ /.muh-KAN-iks/

Mechanics who work on the big engines in tractor-trailer trucks, locomotives, bulldozers, and other industrial or farm vehicles are called diesel mechanics. Diesel engines are stronger than gasoline engines and are used in heavy vehicles and equipment. These mechanics inspect parts, make repairs, and sometimes re-build engines. They may work for trucking companies, buslines, shipyards, and construction firms. Some mechanics specialize in passenger car diesel engines and are employed by automobile firms.

Dietitians and Nutritionists

/DYE-uh-TISH-uns/ and /new-TRISH-un-ists/

Dietitians and nutritionists study how our bodies use the foods we eat. They help people choose foods that will keep the body healthy. They teach about the basic food groups, vitamins and minerals, fats and fiber. They also plan special meals for patients in hospitals. Dietitians and nutritionists are in charge of planning the menus for cafeterias in schools, prisons, rest homes, and other places. They make sure that kitchens and cooking equipment are kept very clean. Nutritionists may specialize in one area, like helping hospitals care for patients.

Directors, Religious Activities and Education

/dih-**REC**-ters/ /rih-**LIJ**-us/ /ac-**TIV**-uh-tees/ and /**ED**-u-**KAY**-shun/

Religious directors plan religious education programs. They lead many religious or church-related activities. Churches may have leaders for music, education, religious school, youth groups, and prayer groups. Some have counselors for dating, marriage, and other personal or religious problems.

Dispatchers

/dih-**SPACH**-ers/

Dispatchers send information out promptly. To send and receive messages, they use communications equipment such as telephones, radios, computers, and fax machines. They keep trains, buses, trucks, planes, and ships on schedule. They also work for police and fire departments, rescue squads, and ambulance and other emergency services. When there is an emergency, dispatchers take information and send help.

Dispensing Opticians

/dis-**PENS**-ing/ /op-**TISH**-uns/

Dispensing opticians provide eyeglasses and contact lenses for people who have had their eyes examined by physicians. Like a pharmacist, a dispensing optician fills the prescription written by the eye doctor. Dispensing opticians keep a large selection of frames and help people choose suitable ones. They also fit contact lenses to people's eyes. When eyeglasses break or need adjusting, opticians provide services.

Drafters

/DRAFF-ters/

Drafters prepare detailed drawings of the plans for buildings, cars, bridges, and other things. They work from the plans or designs of architects, engineers, and scientists to make the drawings or blueprints. Drafters use computer programs to make their drawings.

Drywall Workers and Lathers

/DRY-wall/ /WER-kers/ and /LAY-therz/

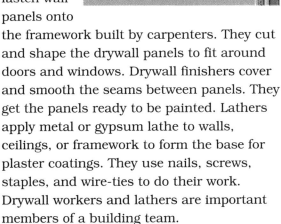

Drywall applicators and finishers install the materials used for walls and ceilings in new homes and buildings. Drywall applicators fasten wall panels onto the framework built by carpenters. They cut and shape the drywall panels to fit around doors and windows. Drywall finishers cover and smooth the seams between panels. They get the panels ready to be painted. Lathers apply metal or gypsum lathe to walls, ceilings, or framework to form the base for plaster coatings. They use nails, screws, staples, and wire-ties to do their work. Drywall workers and lathers are important members of a building team.

Duplicating, Mail, and Other Office Workers

/DOO-plih-KAY-ting/ /mail/ and other /OFF-iss/ /WER-kers/

Office workers do many things in large and busy workplaces. Mail clerks sort and deliver all the mail. They prepare mailing lists and make sure they are up-to-date. They also pack and mail products to customers. Some workers operate different types of copy machines. Office workers may file papers, answer telephones, locate materials, use computers, and make schedules.

Economists

/ee-**CON**-uh-mists/

Economists study the many ways a society produces, buys, and sells things. They are interested in how much things cost, how much workers are paid, and how much money is borrowed or loaned by banks. Economists help businesses and governments prepare budgets. They use charts and tables of numbers. They try to explain money problems and trends such as inflation and unemployment.

Education Administrators

/**ED**-u-**KAY**-shun/
/ad-**MIN**-iss-**TRAY**-ters/

Education administrators are the leaders and managers of schools and school systems. They are in charge of the teachers, programs, buildings, money, and many other services involved in educating young people in elementary and secondary schools. Superintendents, principals, and curriculum leaders are school administrators. In colleges and universities, the administrators are known as deans, provosts, presidents, and assistants.

EEG Technologists and Technicians

EEG /tek-**NOL**-uh-jists/ and /tek-**NISH**-uns/

EEG technologists and technicians operate machines that read and record brain waves. These waves are patterns of electrical activity that occur as the brain gives and receives information that controls all parts of the body. Doctors use the records to decide if the brain has been injured by disease or in accidents. The machine used to read brain waves is called an electroencephalograph. EEG is an abbreviation of this long word.

EKG Technicians

EKG /tek-**NISH**-uns/

EKG technicians operate machines that read and record the activities of the heart. These records are used by doctors to decide if the heart is diseased or if the rhythm of heartbeats is too slow or too fast. EKG technicians attach wires called electrodes to a person's chest and these wires send signals to the machines. EKG is an abbreviation for the name of this machine, an electrocardiograph.

Electrical and Electronics Engineers

/ee-**LEC**-tri-kul/ and /ee-lec-**TRON**-ics/ /**EN**-ji-**NEERS**/

Electrical and electronics engineers plan, test, and help build many kinds of electrical and electronic equipment. Their designs are used by power companies, in cars, and in lighting and wiring systems for buildings. They design appliances and all machines run by electricity. Televisions, computers, and robots are other things designed by electrical engineers.

Electric Power Generating Plant Operators and Power Distributors and Dispatchers

/ee-**LEC**-tric/ /**POW**-er/ /**JEN**-er-**ATE**-ing/ /plant/ /**OP**-er-**ATE**-ers/ and /**POW**-er/ /dis-**TRIB**-u-ters/ and /dih-**SPACH**-ers/

Electricity for our homes and communities is generated, or produced, in plants where water, coal, nuclear energy, wind power, or energy from the sun turns giant turbine engines. Operators carefully and skillfully monitor, check, control, and keep records on the many types of equipment used in power plants. Distributors and dispatchers operate equipment that controls the flow of electric power from the plant through the lines into our homes, schools, and office buildings.

Electronic Home Entertainment Equipment Repairers

/ee-lec-**TRON**-ic/ /home/ /**ENT**-er-**TAIN**-ment/ /ee-**KWIP**-ment/ /re-**PAIR**-ers/

Electronic home entertainment equipment repairers work on many types of audio and video equipment. Along with televisions, DVD players, and VCRs, they also repair stereo equipment, radios, tape recorders, video games, video cameras, CD players, MP3 players, and home computers. They check for worn-out parts and wires. They replace faulty connections and circuits. They follow service manuals and wiring diagrams and must be knowledgeable about electronics.

Electricians

/ee-lec-**TRISH**-uns/

Electricians assemble, install, and maintain electrical systems in homes, office buildings, and factories. These systems are needed to operate lights, heating and air conditioning units, appliances, and tools that run on electrical power. Electricians follow blueprints and codes. They install wires, cables, circuits, and switches during construction. They use handtools such as pliers, screwdrivers, and knives, power tools, and test meters.

Elevator Installers and Repairers

/**EL**-eh-**VAY**-ter/ /in-**STALL**-ers/ and /re-**PAIR**-ers/

Companies that make elevators need skilled workers to install them in buildings and to keep them in good working order. Installers and repairers must know all the parts of an elevator, from the counterweight to the cables to the electrical control system. All of the parts must be checked, adjusted, and tested on a regular schedule to assure the safety of elevator passengers.

Emergency Medical Technicians

/ee-**MER**-jen-see/ /**MED**-ih-kul/ /tek-**NISH**-uns/

Emergency medical technicians are often called EMTs. They work for rescue squads, ambulance services, hospitals, or fire and police departments. They rush to the scene of accidents and other emergencies and take care of injured or sick people. EMTs apply life-saving measures until they can get victims to a hospital for further treatment. They must also keep their emergency vehicles and medical equipment in good working order.

Employment Interviewers

/em-**PLOY**-ment/
/**IN**-ter-**VIEW**-ers/

Finding the most qualified person to perform a particular job is a process. One of the steps in the process is interviewing the different people who apply for a job. Interviewers ask questions about a person's interests, skills, work experience, expectations, and attitudes. Some work for employment firms which help match just the right workers to the right jobs. Others work in the personnel section of large companies that recruit and hire their own employees.

Engineering, Science, and Computer Systems Managers

/**EN**-ji-**NEER**-ing/ /**SY**-ence/ and /com-**PEW**-ter/ /**SIS**-tems/ /**MAN**-uh-jers/

These managers plan and direct technical and scientific work. They supervise engineers, scientists, or data processing workers who design new products, new ways of working, or new research projects. Managers make detailed plans, determine costs, and arrange for the work to be done. Most work in offices but some may work in plants. A few managers are in charge of large laboratories.

Farm Equipment Mechanics

/farm/ /ee-**KWIP**-ment/ /muh-**KAN**-iks/

Farm equipment mechanics service and repair machines used in farming. They work on tractors, harvesting combines, hay balers, or corn pickers. They test, adjust, and clean parts and tune engines of these machines. Farm equipment mechanics are very busy during planting and harvesting seasons. Many are employed by dealers who sell equipment to farmers. Some mechanics manage their own repair shops.

Farmers and Farm Managers

/**FARM**-ers/ and /farm/ /**MAN**-uh-jers/

Farmers and farm managers plant and harvest the crops and raise the animals that supply people with food and clothing. They grow many different kinds of fruits and vegetables. They also grow grains, cotton, and plants such as hay or alfalfa used to feed livestock. Farmers raise beef cattle, pigs, sheep, and chickens. They spend much of their time keeping equipment, farms, and fences in good order. They work to keep plants and animals healthy. And, as farming is a business, they keep accounts and records. Farm managers are hired on large farms to do general planning, planting and harvesting, and marketing or storing crops.

Fashion Designers/Consultants

/**FASH**-un/ /dee-**ZINE**-ers/ /con-**SUL**-tants/

Fashion designers create new styles of clothing for people to wear. They design coats, suits, dresses, skirts, pants, sweaters, and shoes. Also, they design fashion accessories, which are things like belts, scarves, and jewelry. They make drawings or sketches of their ideas. Sometimes they search for or even design colorful and interesting fabrics. Some fashion designers work alone and others design for companies that make clothes. Fashion consultants help people decide what they should wear. Many work in stores, where they help customers pick out colors and clothing styles that look best on them.

Fast Food Workers

/fast/ /food/ /WER-kers/

These employees work in fast food restaurants and help customers in many ways. Some take orders at the counter or at the drive-through window. They may also cook, package the order, make coffee, and pour drinks from a machine. Workers also deliver the drinks and food to customers and take payment. There are usually many jobs available. Workers who have experience and training can become managers.

Financial Managers

/fy-NAN-chul/ /MAN-uh-jers/

Most organizations or businesses that make money have a financial manager to keep track of it. Financial managers maintain records of operating expenses, taxes, salaries and benefits, income, and profit. Some financial managers work for individuals who need help investing their money. Others may work for farmers and business owners who want to increase their profits. Financial managers also work as banking and loan officers.

Firefighters

/FIRE-FYTE-ers/

Firefighters work to prevent fires and to save people's lives and property when fires do happen. Putting out a fire takes teamwork. Some firefighters drive the fire engines, connect the water hoses, or set up the ladders. Others rescue people or break doors and windows to let out smoke. Firefighters also teach people about fire safety. They inspect buildings for possible fire hazards.

Fishers, Hunters, and Trappers

/FISH-ers/ /HUNT-ers/ and /TRAP-ers/

Most people who like to hunt and fish do it for fun. But some make hunting and fishing a full-time job. Most commercial fishers, hunters, and trappers sell what they catch to restaurants, zoos, museums, and furriers. Some work as guides, taking clients fishing or hunting. Federal, state, and local agencies regulate these activities closely. Some of these workers help with animal damage and disease control.

Fitness and Strength Trainers

/FIT-ness/ and /strength/ /TRAY-ners/

These trainers instruct and coach people or groups in all kinds of fitness activities and exercises. They help people test themselves to find out how healthy and strong they are. Then they help decide what exercises they should do to be even healthier and stronger. They might work in a health club or a gym, or in a school, teaching people how exercise machines work and how exercises are done. Strength trainers help people mostly with lifting weights, but fitness trainers might help with yoga, aerobics, karate, or almost any sport you can imagine!

Flight Attendants

/flite/ /uh-TEN-dants/

Flight attendants (also called stewardesses and stewards) are responsible for the comfort and safety of passengers on airplanes. They greet people boarding the plane, check tickets and seat assignments, and serve food and beverages. Flight attendants also check to see that seatbelts are fastened. They teach passengers how to use emergency equipment. If passengers become ill, they help them and administer first aid. Flight attendants wear airline company uniforms and must be able to travel most of the time.

Foresters and Conservation Scientists

/FOR-es-ters/ and /CON-ser-VAY-shun/ /SY-en-tists/

Foresters and conservation scientists are in charge of forests. They help take care of forests, rangelands, and national parks. They are concerned about trees, soil, water, and other natural resources. They also work to protect the wildlife in these areas. Some foresters work for timber companies which plant and harvest trees for lumber. Some are in charge of campgrounds. Others work with crews that fight forest fires. Conservationist scientists help farmers and ranchers make the best use of their land. They work to prevent loss of soil by erosion.

Funeral Directors

/FEW-nuh-rul/
/dih-REC-ters/

When someone dies, it's a very special job helping a family take care of the person they've lost. So a funeral director must enjoy working with people, and must work with them during their saddest time. People who follow different religions, or who come from different countries, have different ways of taking care of loved ones who have died. And a funeral director must know all the different ways, so that he or she can do the best job of helping the family. The body must be prepared for burial or cremation. People will visit with the family, and with the person who has died, one last time, to "pay their respects." And the body must be taken to where it will be buried or cremated. It's up to the funeral director to arrange all of these things and make sure they happen just the way the family wishes.

Gardeners and Groundskeepers

/GARD-en-ers/ and
/GROUNDS-keep-ers/

Think of all the places outdoors that need daily care and maintenance. These are parks, lawns, golf courses, cemeteries, playground and sports fields, and arboretums. Groundskeepers plant trees, shrubs, grass, and flowers. They prune and trim, water, fertilize, mulch, mow, and rake. Gardeners take care of fruit trees and herb, vegetable, and flower gardens. They may also work at historic sites and on large estates.

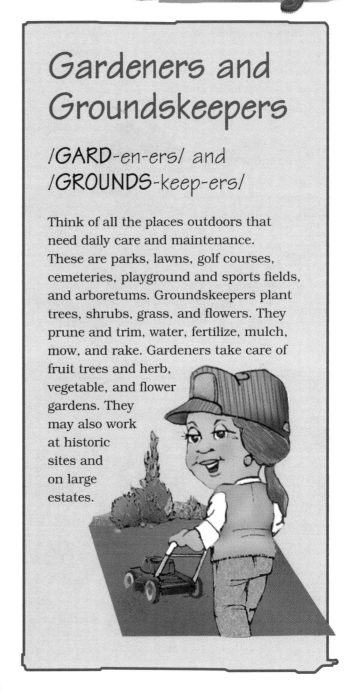

General Maintenance Mechanics

/JEN-er-ul/ /MAYN-teh-nance/ /muh-KAN-iks/

Just like your home, schools, factories, stores, and other places are full of things that require attention. Electrical systems, plumbing, heating and air conditioning units, machines, and equipment all need to be kept in good working order. General maintenance mechanics know how to do many kinds of jobs. They know which parts and tools are needed for repairs. They know when equipment needs to be checked, repaired, or replaced.

General Managers and Top Executives

/JEN-er-ul/ /MAN-uh-jers/ and /top/ /ek-ZEK-kew-tivs/

Managers or executives are in charge of organizations. These include businesses and industries, schools and colleges, government agencies, hospitals, and museums. Being the leader of an organization means being responsible for important decisions, planning, delegating, and solving problems. They must also know about the kind of work that is done and the employees who do it.

General Office Clerks

/JEN-er-ul/ /OFF-iss/ /clerks/

In every business, large or small, many different tasks must be done in the office. General office clerks keep the entire operation running smoothly. They handle many tasks in an organized and efficient manner. They keep records and maintain files. They type or word process letters, orders, and reports. They answer the telephone and talk with customers. General office clerks use machines such as calculators, copy machines, word processors, and telephone switchboards.

Geographers

/gee-**OG**-ra-fers/

Geographers study the earth's landforms and climates. They also study where and how people live. Physical geographers study such things as weather and wind patterns, landscapes, and soils. They learn about how plants and animals live at the different latitudes and longitudes of the earth. Social geographers study the ways people use land, water, and natural resources. They learn how people are affected by where they live on earth.

Geologists

/gee-**OL**-uh-jists/

Geologists study the rocks of which the earth, the moon, and other planets are made. They try to find out how different types of rocks are formed. They study about how old rocks are and where different kinds are located. Geologists also search for oil, gas, and mineral deposits under the soil. They study the layers beneath the surface of the land. These scientists also study fossils, volcanoes, earthquakes, and glaciers.

Geophysicists

/**GEE**-o-**FIZZ**-ih-sists/

Geophysicists study the force of gravity, the magnetic field, and the shape and atmosphere of the earth. They study ocean tides and currents. Geophysicists must know mathematics, physics, and geology to do their work. They use equipment such as seismographs and computers to find out about earth movements such as earthquakes. Geophysicists help geologists search for oil, gas, and mineral deposits. They help them plan ways to explore deep within the earth's crust.

Glaziers

/GLAY-zhers/

Glaziers measure, cut, and install glass used in windows, doors, windshields, and mirrors. Some glaziers use cranes and hoists to do their work. Some stand on tall scaffolding to put the windows in skyscrapers. Others build stained glass windows for churches. Glaziers use hand tools and power tools such as cutters, grinders, and polishers. They replace broken windows and windshields, too.

Graphic Artists

/GRAF-ic/ /AR-tists/

Graphic artists design and illustrate advertisements in newspapers, magazines, and television. They also design book and CD covers, pamphlets, and displays in museums. Some of them think of new wallpaper patterns or create greeting cards or labels for cans. These artists use their talents and creative ideas to deliver a message about products. Their drawings and sketches may give information or make products look good to customers. Graphic artists may create their art by hand or by using a computer.

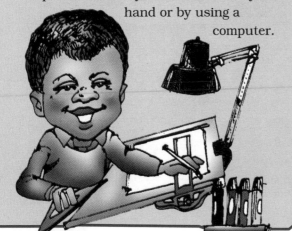

Government Chief Executives and Legislators

/GOV-urn-ment/ /cheef/ /ek-ZEK-kew-tivs/ and /LEJ-is-LATE-ers/

In government, the main leaders are the president and vice president, state governors, and lieutenant governors. Titles of other government leaders are county commissioners, township supervisors, mayors, and city managers. These leaders follow laws in doing their work. They make plans, prepare budgets, and direct the work of government. Men and women who make laws are called legislators. They are senators and representatives in Congress or state legislatures. Sometimes these lawmakers are called assemblymen or delegates. At local levels, they are called council members, aldermen, and selectmen.

Handlers, Equipment Cleaners, Helpers, and Laborers

/HAND-lers/ /ee-KWIP-ment/ /CLEEN-ers/ /HELP-ers/ and /LAY-ber-ers/

These workers are hired at the job-entry level to help more skilled workers. Work includes things such as moving boxes, cleaning equipment or work areas, and loading and unloading materials. Sometimes they use carts, handtrucks, forklifts, or dollies. In grocery stores, they stock shelves, bag groceries, and carry packages to customers' cars. Helpers may assist mechanics or repairers. Some help carpenters, electricians, masons, plumbers, and other construction workers. Some laborers collect trash and garbage and drive garbage trucks.

Health and Regulatory Inspectors

/health/ and /REG-u-la-TOR-ee/ /in-SPEK-ters/

Health and regulatory inspectors help keep people safe and healthy. They work for all levels of government. They check to make sure that rules and laws are being followed. Food inspectors check to see that places where food is packaged and kitchens where food is cooked and served are clean. Transportation inspectors make sure that planes and trains are safe. Some inspectors look for safety problems in factories and mines. Others inspect medicines, sewage plants, water supplies, or hospitals.

Health Services Managers

/health/ /SER-vis-es/ /MAN-uh-jers/

Health services managers plan, organize, and manage places offering health care. They are in charge of hospitals, clinics, and state and local health departments. Some are responsible for hiring doctors, nurses, and other people on the staff. Others handle the financial duties such as paychecks. They order supplies and equipment. Like all managers, those in health services must have leadership skills and the ability to make decisions.

Heating, Air Conditioning, and Refrigeration Mechanics

/HEE-ting/ /air/ /con-DIH-shun-ing/ and /ree-FRIJ-er-AY-shun/ /muh-KAN-iks/

Mechanics for air conditioning, refrigeration, and heating install and service this machinery in homes, factories, and other buildings. They install air conditioners and furnaces as well as pipes, ducts, and electrical wires. Some heating mechanics also repair stoves, clothes dryers, and hot water heaters. Refrigeration mechanics also work with the room-size coolers and freezers in restaurants and meat-packing plants.

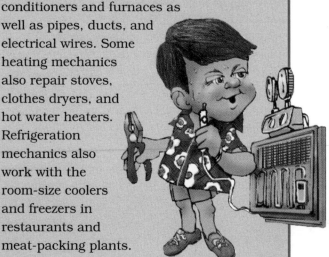

Historians

/hiss-TOR-ee-uns/

Historians study and teach others about how people lived in the past. They often choose to study a certain country, group of people, time in history, or even one person. Then they try to learn all they can about their area of interest. Historians write books and articles and teach in schools and universities. Some work for museums. Archivists are historians who take care of important documents and artifacts. Historians also help preserve historic buildings such as George Washington's house or the Egyptian pyramids. They also help people trace family histories.

Home Appliance and Power Tool Repairers

/home/ /uh-**PLY**-ance/ and /**POW**-er/ /tool/ /re-**PAIR**-ers/

Home appliance and power tool repairers work with machines like toasters, microwave ovens, and refrigerators. They help people hook-up dishwashers and washing machines. They fix broken vacuum cleaners or clothes dryers. To work on appliances, they must know a lot about electricity and motors. Some of them work in appliance repair shops. Others carry their tools in a truck and go to a person's house to work. With all the different kinds of appliances people use in their homes today, people who install and repair appliances are busy in every community.

Home Health Aides

/home/ /health/ /aids/

Instead of staying in a hospital or extended-care home, many sick, disabled, and elderly people stay in their own homes or live with relatives. If they are unable to care for themselves, they depend on a home-healthcare team. This team includes doctors, nurses, social workers, and home health aides. Home health aides help with shopping, cooking, laundry, and other household chores. They also help their patients exercise, take medicines properly, get from a bed into a wheelchair, and take baths.

Hosts and Hostesses

/hosts/ and /**HOS**-tes-es/

Hosts (men) and hostesses (women) welcome customers as they enter a restaurant. They escort people to their tables and give them menus. They keep track of tables that are reserved and others that are available for walk-in customers. They also take reservations, arrange parties, organize special services, and may collect money. These workers may dress up for the job and often work at different times during the week.

Hotel and Motel Desk Clerks

/ho-**TEL**/ and /mo-**TEL** /desk/ /clerks/

Hotel and motel desk clerks provide many services to people staying in hotels, motels, and inns. They work behind the main desk, registering guests, assigning rooms, and checking out keys. Hotel and motel desk clerks also answer telephones, make reservations, and take messages. They handle money and keep records.

Hotel and Motel Managers and Assistants

/ho-**TEL**/ and /mo-**TEL**/
/**MAN**-uh-jers/ and
/uh-**SIS**-tents/

These managers are in charge of hotels, motels, or inns. They hire and supervise other workers such as desk clerks, housekeepers, and bellhops. Managers see that the plumbing, heating, and cooling systems are working. And they make sure the building and parking areas are in good condition. The main duty of a hotel or motel manager is the comfort and safety of people. Assistants to hotel managers include executive housekeepers who make sure everything is clean and well maintained. There may be front office managers for reservations and room assignments, and convention service managers who take care of meetings and special events.

Human Services Workers

/**HEW**-mun/ /**SER**-vis-es/
/**WER**-kers/

Human services workers hold jobs in many different settings. They may work in group homes and halfway houses or community centers. Some provide services to centers for children and youth or families. Job titles include case management aide, social work assistant, residential counselor, community outreach worker, and aid to elderly persons. Job duties vary, depending on the particular person or group of people needing services. Human services workers also keep records and make reports of how many people need and receive services.

Hydrologists

/hy-**DROL**-uh-jists/

Hydrologists are water specialists. Their work is closely related to that of scientists like geologists and geographers. They find and map the locations of surface water and underground water supplies. They study the water in lakes, rivers, and oceans as well as in underground springs. Some hydrologists keep records about the amount of rain that falls. They observe how quickly rainwater is absorbed by soil or is evaporated by the sun. Others work on water problems such as floods and soil erosion.

Industrial Designers

/in-**DUS**-tree-ul/
/dee-**ZINE**-ers/

Industrial designers plan new products and change old ones. In their work they combine artistic talent and knowledge of materials and machines. Industrial designers think of interesting shapes, colors, or features for manufactured products. These include things such as cars, refrigerators, furniture, computers, and toys. They design eye-catching packages and displays for products, too.

Industrial Engineers

/in-**DUS**-tree-ul/ /**EN**-ji-**NEERS**/

Industrial engineers decide how a product can be made in large quantities after it has been designed. They plan the best ways to use materials, machines, energy, and workers to make the product. They are especially concerned with planning the quickest and least costly production method. Most industrial engineers work for industries. Some conduct research or teach.

Industrial Machinery Repairers

/in-DUS-tree-ul/ /muh-SHEEN-er-ee/ /re-PAIR-ers/

Industrial machine repairers keep machines in good working order. They work in plants and factories. When machines break down, they find the problem, and make repairs or replace parts. Their main job is to prevent breakdowns. Sometimes they are called maintenance mechanics. They inspect machines, clean them, and grease and oil the parts. Repairers work in all factories where machinery is used to make products. These products include textiles, printing, cars, and food such as doughnuts or cookies.

Industrial Production Managers

/in-DUS-tree-ul/ /pro-DUC-shun/ /MAN-uh-jers/

Factories are places where goods are produced. Managers are needed to oversee the workers who operate industrial machinery and equipment to produce goods in the factories. They direct the work being done and handle problems that may arise. In large plants with several operations, there are managers in charge of each operation such as machining, assembly, or finishing. These managers are concerned with making good products and the costs of production. They often meet with managers of other departments, such as sales or traffic, to discuss production goals.

Industrial Truck Operators

/in-DUS-tree-ul/ /truck/ /OP-er-ATE-ers/

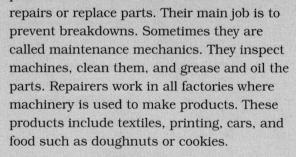

Industrial truck operators drive the power trucks used to lift and move heavy materials. You would find them working in large plants and factories. The trucks have forklifts to pick up stacks of supplies or cartons. The forklift can be used to place things on high storage shelves. Some trucks have tow bars and other special attachments. The industrial truck operators must use care and skill in driving. They should not allow materials to be damaged.

Information Clerks

/IN-for-MAY-shun/ /clerks/

Information clerks use computers to do their work. They collect, organize, interpret, and classify information. When entered in the computer, the information is called a "database". Information clerks may work for libraries, small and large businesses, schools, governments, and hospitals.

Inspectors, Testers, and Graders

/in-SPEK-ters/ /TEST-ers/ and /GRADE-ers/

People need high-quality products. Inspectors, testers, and graders make sure that quality products are available. Nearly all manufactured products are inspected, including products such as foods, clothing, and cars. They may touch products, listen to products, smell them or even taste them. They look for imperfections such as cuts, scratches, missing pieces, or crooked seams. Many holders of these jobs use tools, gauges, and test machinery. Some use electronic equipment, calipers, and other instruments. They mark or make notes of problems. If a product passes inspection, it may have a stamp or number on it to show it was checked.

Insulation Workers

/IN-suh-LAY-shun/ /WER-kers/

Insulation workers install special materials in homes and buildings to save energy. Insulation is placed between walls, under floors, and under roofs. It keeps warm air from escaping on cold days and cool air from escaping on warm days. Insulation is often wrapped around water pipes and air ducts.

Insulation workers measure, cut, paste, staple, wire, tape, and spray these materials. They use cork, felt, fiberglass, tar paper, and spray foam in their work.

Insurance Agents and Brokers

/in-SUR-ance/ /A-jentz/ and /BRO-kers/

Insurance sales workers are called agents and brokers. They sell insurance policies to individuals and companies. They help people plan how to pay for emergencies and losses. For a yearly fee or premium, the insurance company will pay if a house is destroyed by fire or a car needs repairs after an accident. Agents work for just one insurance company. Brokers compare the policies and prices of several companies so the buyer can choose.

Interior Designers/ Decorators

/in-TEER-ee-er/ /dee-ZINE-ers/ /DEK-o-RATE-ers/

Whenever you walk into a hotel or a restaurant—and many houses too—you can bet that the furniture, lights, rugs, and everything else you see were put there by an interior designer or interior decorator. Some of them work alone. Or they may work for a big design company, or even the company that built the house or office. They meet with home owners, owners of restaurants and offices, and others, to find out what they want their home or business to look like on the inside. Then they pick out furniture, pillows, lamps, and everything else needed to make the place look its best. Many of them "draw" the room first on a computer, or they may draw it by hand, pasting up fabric swatches and wood samples so you can see what they plan to do.

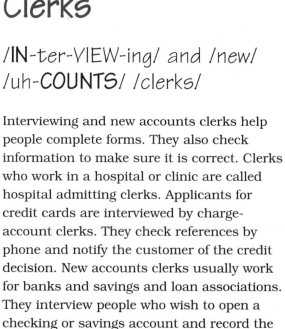

Interviewing and New Accounts Clerks

/IN-ter-VIEW-ing/ and /new/ /uh-COUNTS/ /clerks/

Interviewing and new accounts clerks help people complete forms. They also check information to make sure it is correct. Clerks who work in a hospital or clinic are called hospital admitting clerks. Applicants for credit cards are interviewed by charge-account clerks. They check references by phone and notify the customer of the credit decision. New accounts clerks usually work for banks and savings and loan associations. They interview people who wish to open a checking or savings account and record the information on an application form.

Janitors and Cleaners

/JAN-ih-ters/ and /CLEEN-ers/

Janitors and cleaners take care of large buildings such as schools, hotels, hospitals, and offices. They do much more than mop, sweep, vacuum, and empty trash cans. Janitors check the heating and air conditioning systems to make sure the lights are working, and to make repairs. They get rid of insects and mice. Usually, janitors and cleaners work late at night or early in the morning.

Jewelers

/JEW-el-ers/

Jewelers design, make, and repair rings, necklaces, bracelets, earrings, and other jewelry. They use precious metals such as gold and silver. They may use diamonds, rubies, emeralds, and other gemstones. Jewelers shape the metal with hand tools, cast it in molds, and solder (sod-der) pieces together. Jewelers can also repair broken clasps, re-set stones, and change the size of rings.

Judges

/JUD-jes/

Judges are the top officials in federal, state, county, and city courts. They are lawyers who have been elected or appointed to their positions. All judges make decisions on matters of law. They decide what evidence can be used in a trial and which laws a jury must consider when deciding a verdict. Supreme Court judges are also known as justices. They make decisions about violations or interpretations of the United States Constitution.

Kindergarten and Elementary School Teachers

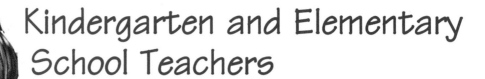

/KIN-der-GAR-ten/ and /EL-eh-MEN-tuh-ree/
/skool/ /TEE-chers/

Kindergarten and elementary school teachers help children learn their lessons. They teach their students to read and to enjoy learning. They help them learn about the world we live in. They teach beginning mathematics, language arts, science, and social studies. Some of them teach art, music, or physical education. Like all teachers, they plan lessons, grade papers, and continue to learn about new ideas and different ways of teaching.

Labor Relations Specialists and Managers

/LAY-ber/ /re-LAY-shuns/
/SPEH-shul-ists/
and /MAN-uh-jers/

Labor relations specialists and managers provide a link between employers and employees. They work for the owners of large companies and with the workers. They protect the rights of workers who are members of a union. Unions organize workers so they can join together to bargain with companies for higher wages and fair treatment in the workplace.

Landscape Architects

/LAND-scape/ /AR-kih-TECS/

Designing outdoor areas requires knowledge of how people will use an area. Landscape architects study what soils, trees, plants, and natural features exist and think about what structures will be built on the site. They work with the planners, architects, and builders of residential and business complexes, parks, recreation facilities, and shopping centers. Their plans often determine the amount of attention given to protecting the environment.

Laundry and Drycleaning Machine Operators and Tenders

/LON-dree/ and /DRY-CLEEN-ing/ /muh-SHEEN/ /OP-er-ATE-ers/ and /TEN-ders/

Laundry and drycleaning machine operators and tenders work in shops where clothing and linens are cleaned. Laundry workers sort clothes by fabrics and colors. They load them into washing machines to be cleaned with soap and water. Or they place things in drycleaning machines with chemical solutions. Some workers specialize in cleaning furs, leather, or silk. Large places like hospitals sometimes operate their own laundries.

Lawyers

/LAW-yers/

Lawyers study to become experts about rules and regulations. These rules or laws help protect the rights of people and businesses. Lawyers help their clients understand the legal system and their rights as citizens. In a trial, lawyers speak for their clients before a judge and jury. Some lawyers help people with business contracts or taxes. Others help with legal documents such as wills and deeds for property. Lawyers are also called attorneys.

Librarians

/ly-BRAIR-ee-uns/

Librarians select and organize books and materials for libraries. They help people find the information they need. They use special letters and numbers called classification systems to label materials and to store information about them in the library's computer system. Some librarians read stories to children. Others are in charge of film, music, or map collections. Most library information, such as orders for new materials, is now kept on computers.

Library Assistants and Bookmobile Drivers

/LY-brair-ee/ /uh-SIS-tents/
and /BOOK-mo-BEEL/ /DRY-vers/

Librarians depend on a variety of helpers to operate a library. Assistants perform many tasks. They shelve books, order new materials, and keep records on the library's computer system telling what books and other materials the library has. They help people locate and check out books, maps, videos, and other resources. Bookmobile drivers deliver a selection of books to people in rural areas or communities without a library building.

Licensed Practical Nurses

/LY-sensed/ /PRAC-tih-kul/
/NURS-es/

Licensed practical nurses (LPNs) help doctors and registered nurses care for medical patients. In hospitals, they bathe and feed patients, and give them their medicine. Some nurses work in nursing homes and doctors' offices. Others help take care of people who are sick at home.

Line Installers and Cable Splicers

/line/ /in-STALL-ers/ and
/CAY-bul/ /SPLYS-ers/

Line installers and cable splicers connect, maintain, and repair wires and lines used for electricity, telephone signals, cable television, and the Internet. Installers set up the poles that carry the cables. Sometimes cables are buried underground and even under the oceans. Splicers join the individual wires together. Then they seal them inside insulated cables. These workers are often called to make emergency repairs when cables are damaged by storms or earthquakes.

Lithographers and Photoengravers

/lith-**OG**-ra-fers/ and
/**FO**-to-en-**GRAY**-vers/

Lithographers and photoengravers work in the printing industry. They make metal plates of the material to be printed. These plates are then smeared with ink and pressed against rubber rollers to transfer the image onto paper. Lithographers and photoengravers use cameras, chemicals, dyes, and engraving tools to do their work.

Machine Repairers

/muh-**SHEEN**/ /re-**PAIR**-ers/

These repairers work with office machines. They keep everything in good working order. They adjust, clean, and oil mechanical and electrical parts and look for loose connections or worn-out circuits. It's important to quickly find the problem and make the needed repairs or replacements. Some work on calculators, cash registers, or duplicating equipment. They may use needle-nosed pliers and soldering (sod-der-ing) guns. Electrical parts must be tested with special equipment.

Machine Tool Operators

/muh-**SHEEN**/ /tool/ /**OP**-er-**ATE**-ers/

Machine tool operators run machines that are used to bend and shape metal and plastic. They work in factories that produce metal and plastic products. They make engine parts, car fenders, and parts for rockets and planes. Machine tool operators work with lathes, milling machines, drill presses, and punch presses. They adjust the speed, feed the pieces of rough metal into the machine, and turn the controls.

Machinists

/muh-**SHEEN**-ists/

Machinists, also called production machine operators, are skilled metalworkers. They set up and operate the equipment used in factories to make metal parts. These parts are for cars, planes, engines, and tools. They shape steel, iron, brass, and aluminum. Some of them make the machines that make parts for other machines. Machinists operate power-driven machines and handtools to cut, drill, and grind pieces of metal.

Mail Carriers and Postal Clerks

/mail/ /**CAIR**-ee-ers/ and /**PO**-stul/ /clerks/

Mail carriers and postal clerks work for the United States Postal Service. Mail carriers travel assigned routes to deliver and collect mail. They work in all kinds of weather. Some walk and others drive small trucks. Postal clerks work in local post offices sorting mail, selling postage stamps, and weighing packages.

Mail Clerks and Messengers

/mail/ /clerks/ and /**MESS**-en-jers/

Large companies and organizations such as colleges and hospitals have mailrooms in which clerks prepare outgoing mail and receive incoming mail. Mail delivered by the U.S. Postal Service as well as inter-departmental mail is sorted and carried to the proper person or office in the building complex. Messengers are called to deliver reports or other information to various locations as quickly as possible.

Management Analysts and Consultants

/MAN-ij-ment/ /AN-uh-lists/ and /con-SUL-tants/

When organizations, government agencies, or businesses decide to make changes or try something new, they often hire management analysts or consultants to help. Since new equipment or different production methods may be very expensive, consultants try to find the best way to make any changes. They talk to the people involved, figure out the costs, and make recommendations. They plan efficient methods and train workers. Consultants must also be good problem-solvers.

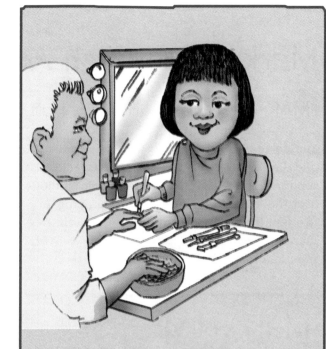

Manicurists

/MAN-ih-KYOOR-ists/

Manicurists have special jobs in beauty shops or hairstyling salons. They work with customers' hands and feet. Manicures include preparing, shaping, and coloring the fingernails. Pedicures are done on the toenails. Manicurists know about skin care as well as healthy nail care. They also meet and must get along with many different people.

Manufacturers' Sales Representatives

/MAN-u-FAK-cher-ers/ /sales/ /REP-pree-ZEN-tuh-tivs/

Manufacturers' sales workers sell their company's products. They sell to factories, businesses, and places such as schools and hospitals. They sell everything from electronic equipment and industrial machines to furniture, food, and computers. These sales workers describe their product, suggest why the buyer should purchase it, and take orders. They travel often and to many places to contact customers.

Market Research Analysts

/MAR-ket/ /REE-surch/ /AN-uh-lists/

Market research analysts collect information. Knowing people's likes and dislikes can be important to companies that make and sell products. First, people are asked their opinions during interviews, over the telephone, when they're shopping, and on questionnaires sent through the mail. Sometimes they are sent free samples to try out. The market researcher analyzes or studies everyone's answers and writes reports and summaries.

Marketing and Advertising Managers

/MAR-ket-ing/ and /AD-ver-TY-zing/ /MAN-uh-jers/

Marketing managers find out the demand for the products and services that their companies make and sell. They also learn how their companies compare with other firms who sell similar products and services. They want their companies to do better than other firms. Advertising managers select the kind of advertising which will help sell products and services. Radio, television, newspapers, magazines, the Internet, and outdoor signs can be used to advertise.

Mathematicians

/MATH-eh-muh-TISH-uns/

Mathematicians use numbers as symbols for the scientific study of measuring things. They develop new ways to measure such things as quantities, distances, shapes, sizes, and amounts of energy. Some mathematicians study and seek new knowledge. Others apply mathematics to business, engineering, and science. Most mathematicians use computers to help do their work solving problems.

Mechanical Engineering Technicians

/muh-**KAN**-ih-kul/ /**EN**-ji-**NEER**-ing/ /tek-**NISH**-uns/

Mechanical engineering technicians help carry out the plans of mechanical engineers. They make drawings of each different part of a machine. And, they help build new power machinery and equipment. These technicians test metals and other materials and help decide if these are the best to use for motor and engine parts. Some technicians also work with the electrical and fuel systems that run the machinery.

Mechanical Engineers

/muh-**KAN**-ih-kul/ /**EN**-ji-**NEERS**/

Mechanical engineers design and help make machines that produce power. These machines include internal combustion engines, steam and gas turbines, and jet and rocket engines. These engineers also design motors and engines for elevators, cars, lawnmowers, and industrial machines. Some mechanical engineers are working on new energy systems that will reduce pollution in the environment.

Medical Assistants

/**MED**-ih-kul/ /uh-**SIS**-tents/

Medical assistants work for physicians, clinics, and hospitals. Some help examine and treat patients. Others perform office duties. Clinical assistants record a patient's weight, height, and blood pressure. They may keep supplies stocked, examining rooms clean, and instruments sterilized. Clerical assistants answer the telephone, make appointments, keep patients' records in order, prepare bills, and fill out insurance forms.

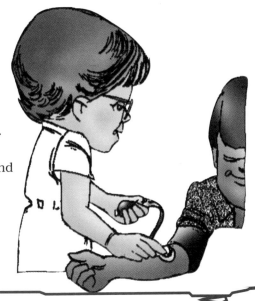

Medical Laboratory Technologists and Technicians

/MED-ih-kul/ /LAB-rah-TOR-ee/ /tek-NOL-uh-jists/ and /tek-NISH-uns/

Medical laboratory technologists and technicians work in hospitals and health clinics. They examine samples of blood, urine, and other body fluids and tissues under a microscope. They look for any changes in the cells which are caused by diseases or bacteria. These laboratory tests help doctors decide what is wrong with their patients and how to treat them.

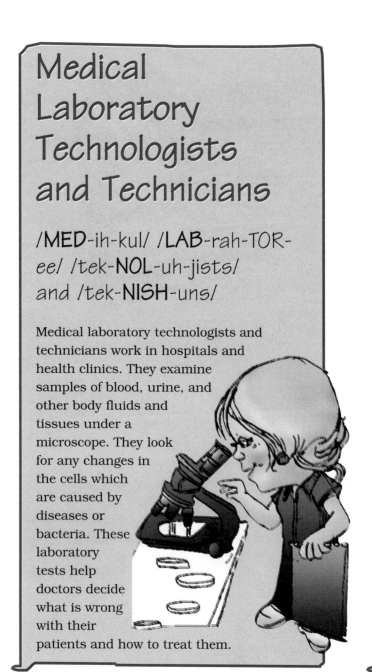

Medical Transcriptionists

/MED-ih-kul/ /tran-SCRIP-shun-ists/

Doctors and other healthcare workers keep careful records when they treat patients. Often, they use special tape recorders and dictate information. Medical transcriptionists listen carefully to the tapes and make written reports for the files. They must be very accurate and write down exactly what is said. Workers must also know all the medical terms and how to spell them correctly.

Metallurgical, Ceramic, and Materials Engineers

/MET-uh-LUR-jih-kul/ /ser-RAM-ic/ and /muh-TEER-ee-uhls/ /EN-ji-NEERS/

Metallurgical, ceramic, and materials engineers develop new materials that resist heat or that are strong but light in weight. Metallurgical engineers work with metals. They mine ore from the ground, refine it, and make metals and alloys. Ceramic engineers develop new ceramic materials and create products. Materials engineers select just the right materials to use in many new and familiar products.

Meteorologists

/MEE-tee-or-OL-uh-jists/

Meteorologists study the earth's climate and the causes of different weather conditions. They examine temperature, humidity, air pressure, clouds, and wind. Meteorologists use photographs taken by satellites, charts and maps, and records of past weather conditions. Meteorologists work in weather stations all over the world and share their observations with each other. Computers are very useful in the work of forecasting and understanding changes in the weather.

Microbiologists

/MY-crow-by-OL-uh-jists/

Microbiologists are scientists. They study living things that are so small they are visible only through a microscope. These include bacteria, viruses, and molds. Some study tiny organisms that live in the water or in dirt. Others are interested in those that live in the human body or in animals and plants. They study both the organisms that cause diseases, and those that fight infections or help digest food. Most microbiologists conduct research in laboratories.

Millwrights

/MILL-rites/

Millwrights install the machinery and heavy equipment used in almost every industry. They put together the spinning and weaving machines in textile plants. They install the big ovens and stoves in food plants, and even build industrial robots. Millwrights assemble all the parts of these machines and the platforms that hold them. They fit bearings, line up gears, attach motors, and connect belts. They also repair equipment and keep it in good working order.

Mining Engineers

/MY-ning/ /EN-ji-NEERS/

Manufacturing industries use minerals. Mining engineers find and remove these mineral deposits from the ground. They work with metallurgical engineers and geologists to locate copper, coal, or phosphates. Engineers design and help build underground mine shafts and tunnels. They also design and build mining equipment. Some mining engineers study ways to better separate minerals from dirt, rock, and other materials.

Mobile Heavy Equipment Mechanics

/MO-bill/ /HEV-ee/ /ee-KWIP-ment/ /muh-KAN-iks/

Many construction jobs, logging, mining, and road building companies require heavy equipment like bulldozers, motor graders, backhoes, concrete mixers, cranes, and crawler-loaders. Mobile heavy equipment mechanics maintain and repair this equipment. These mechanics know how to fix hydraulic systems, electronic parts, and parts that need welding.

Motorcycle, Boat, and Small Engine Mechanics

/MO-ter-SY-kul/ /boat/ and /small/ EN-jin /muh-KAN-iks/

Think of all the machines that are powered by small gasoline engines. Some examples are lawnmowers, chain saws, soil tillers, outboard boat motors, and jet skis. When these engines break down, mechanics figure out the problem, order or repair parts, and fix the engines. Some mechanics specialize in certain kinds of engines such as those that power motorcycles.

Musical Instrument Repairers and Tuners

/MU-zih-kul/ /IN-struh-ment/ /re-PAIR-ers/ and /TOON-ers/

Musical instrument repairers adjust, tune, and repair the many kinds of instruments used by musicians. Piano tuners set all the strings inside the piano at their proper pitch. They use tuning forks and tuning levers or wrenches. Pipe-organ tuners use tuning forks and metal slides to match the pitch of pipes. A reed pipe is tuned by changing the length of the brass reed inside the pipe. Repairers also install the large organs in churches. Other musical instrument repairers work on violins, trumpets, clarinets, and other instruments. They repair cracks in wood, solder (sod-der) metal, and replace strings.

Musicians and Singers

/mu-ZIH-shuns/ and /SING-ers/

Musicians create and perform music. They use string, brass, woodwind, or percussion instruments. They are paid to entertain people by making music in symphony orchestras, concerts, dance or marching bands, rock groups, and jazz ensembles. Some musicians use their voices to entertain people. They sing different types of music, too, such as opera, rock, folk, or country and western. Musicians also accompany singers and dancers. Some teach music. Learning to sing or play a musical instrument takes years of study and practice.

Network and Computer Systems Administrators

/NET-werk/ and /com-PEW-ter/ /SIS-tems/ /ad-MIN-iss-TRAY-ters/

People who work for the same company can talk to each other and share things through their computers. Their computers are all connected on a "network", and someone has to keep the network running smoothly. That's the job of a network and computer systems administrator. They make sure that all the company's computers and software work the way they should, so that everyone can get information and share information to do their jobs.

Nuclear Engineers

/NEW-clee-er/ /EN-ji-NEERS/

Nuclear engineers plan and help build and operate nuclear power plants used to make electricity. Some of them also work on nuclear weapons. Since making nuclear energy produces dangerous radioactive waste materials, nuclear engineers also work to find safe ways to get rid of this waste. Other nuclear engineers work for companies or laboratories that conduct medical research.

Nuclear Medicine Technologists

/NEW-clee-er / /MED-ih-sin/ /tek-NOL-uh-jists/

Nuclear medicine uses radioactive materials to find and treat diseases. Patients either swallow these materials or receive an injection. Technologists trace them using special tools called scanners. Besides providing the chemicals and using the scanners, technicians must also explain to patients what will happen. Radioactive chemicals are very dangerous so technicians must follow strict safety rules.

Numerical Control Machine-Tool Operators

/new-MAIR-ih-kul/ /con-TROL/ /muh-SHEEN/ /tool/ /OP-er-ATE-ers/

These workers operate machines which cut or form metal or plastic workpieces into parts for products. The operators set up and properly use these machines which are controlled by a computer. The machines automate the production of the parts needed. Some operators tend only one machine. Other operators may operate more than one machine at a time. They may also operate different types of machines.

Nursing Aides and Psychiatric Aides

/**NUR**-sing/ /aids/ and /**SY**-kee-**AT**-trik/ /aids/

Nursing aides and psychiatric aides help care for physically or mentally ill patients in hospitals and nursing homes. Some aides also help sick or elderly people in their homes. This group of helpers performs many necessary tasks. They serve meals, feed patients unable to feed themselves, bathe and dress patients, and change bed linens. They also bring supplies and medicines to the nurses and help move patients in wheelchairs or on rolling beds. Psychiatric aides care for mentally impaired or emotionally disturbed individuals. They try to interest patients in activities which will help the patients change their behavior.

Occupational Therapists

/**OC**-cu-**PAY**-shun-ul/ /**THAIR**-uh-pists/

Occupational therapists help people who have been injured in accidents or who are recovering from serious illnesses or operations. People who lose a hand, their sight, or who must use a wheelchair can learn from an occupational therapist. They may learn things to help them adjust to this change in their lives. They can learn new job skills, exercises, new ways to cook, bathe, and dress, and how to take care of themselves.

Operations Research Analysts

/**OP**-per-**RAY**-shuns/ /**REE**-surch/ /**AN**-uh-lists/

Like other types of consultants or analysts, these workers are problem solvers. They help the companies that hire them save time and money. They study the company's current way of operating, conduct research into better methods, and re-design the steps in the process. They often use computers in their work and train hundreds of employees.

Ophthalmic Laboratory Technicians

/ahf-THAL-mik/ /LAB-rah-TOR-ee/ /tek-NISH-uns/

Ophthalmic laboratory technicians make eyeglasses and contact lenses. They cut, grind, and polish lenses according to exact measurements and prescriptions. Then they assemble the lenses and frames. Ophthalmic laboratory technicians use special tools such as glass cutters and drills, files, pliers, and other precision instruments.

Optometrists

/op-TOM-uh-TRISTS/

Optometrists examine people's eyes and prescribe eyeglasses or eye exercises to improve vision. They also check for diseases and refer people to ophthalmologists, or doctors who treat eye diseases and perform eye surgery. Optometrists use special machines to examine, test, and measure vision.

Order Clerks

/OR-der/ /clerks/

Order clerks take orders for materials, goods, or services. Sometimes they are called customer-order clerks, order fillers, or order takers. Most work with computers. If there are questions about an order, order clerks make sure they find out what the customer wants. Clerks must keep track of how many items are left. Sometimes they make reports to managers.

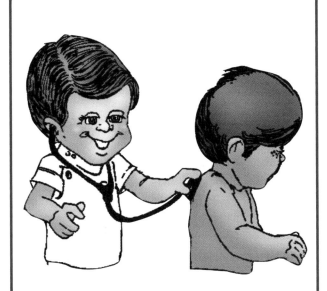

Osteopathic Physicians

/AH-stee-o-**PATH**-ik/
/fih-**ZISH**-uns/

Osteopathic physicians are doctors who work with bones, muscles, ligaments, and nerves. They treat patients by using surgery, medicine, exercises, special diets, and other things. Some doctors teach, do research, and write or edit scientific books and journals. Most are "family doctors" who help patients with other medical problems, as well.

Painters and Paperhangers

/**PAYNT**-ers/ and
/**PAY**-per-**HANG**-ers/

Painters and paperhangers give the finishing touches to the walls and ceilings of buildings. Painters use brushes, rollers, and spray guns to apply paint. They also paint, stain, and varnish the outside of buildings to protect them from the weather. Painters mix paints and match colors. Paperhangers apply wallpaper and other decorative materials. They must measure and cut very carefully.

Paralegals

/**PAIR**-uh-**LEE**-guls/

Paralegals are also called legal assistants. They help lawyers write documents and prepare cases for trial. They research and investigate, write reports, and keep records and files in order. Paralegals do not need to know as much about the law as lawyers do, but they must have a general understanding of the legal system. Some may specialize in one type of law.

Pediatricians

/PEE-dee-uh-**TRISH**-uns/

Pediatricians are doctors who work with infants and children. They treat injuries, illnesses, and childhood diseases.

Pediatricians are especially interested in the healthy growth and development of their patients. They check to be sure that bones and muscles are growing properly and that children are eating good foods.

They also work with parents and teach them how to take good care of young children.

Personnel Clerks

/PER-suh-**NEL**/ /clerks/

Personnel clerks work with employee records to keep records in order and up to date. They see that forms are filled out correctly. These forms may be for health and life insurance, tax withholding, and other things. Personnel clerks give new employees information about pay rates and rules of the workplace. Some personnel clerks help with hiring new workers. They interview job applicants and give them information. Sometimes personnel clerks perform reception duties such as answering the telephone and greeting people.

Pharmacists

/FARM-uh-sists/

Pharmacists fill prescriptions for drugs and medicines prescribed by doctors and dentists for their patients. Pharmacists understand the chemical make-up of medicines, the proper dosages, and the effects of different drugs on the body. They are in charge of large supplies of medicine. And, they are responsible for controlling who uses these drugs. Pharmacists keep records of each prescription that is filled.

Photographers and Camera Operators

/fo-TOG-ra-fers/ and /CAM-er-uh/ /OP-er-ATE-ers/

Photographers use cameras to take pictures of many different things. Some of them record images on moving film or video for television and movies. Others take still photographs that are printed in books, magazines, and newspapers. Some photographers work inside studios with special lighting equipment. Some travel to schools, weddings, or special news and sports events. A few photographers develop their own film with chemicals in a darkroom. Camera operators use special cameras to film movies, television programs, and news events, as well as commercials.

Photographic Process Workers

/fo-to-GRAF-ik/
/PRAH-ses/ /WER-kers/

Photographic process workers develop film, make prints and slides, and enlarge or touch-up photographs. Some of them specialize in processing color film. Chemical solutions and lights are used to transfer images from film to special paper. Most film processing is done in photo labs and darkrooms.

Physical Therapists

/FIZZ-ih-kul/ /THAIR-uh-pists/

Physical therapists help people recover from injuries or diseases. They design treatment plans to help people regain their strength and skills. They use exercises, massages, and heat or water therapy. Therapists also teach people with handicaps how to use artificial limbs, wheelchairs, and braces. Most physical therapists work in hospitals or nursing homes.

Physical Therapy Assistants and Aides

/FIZZ-ih-kul/ /THAIR-uh-pee/ /uh-SIS-tents/ and /aids/

Physical therapy assistants and aides work with patients as they exercise to make injured muscles and bones stronger. They help patients follow a treatment plan designed for them by a physical therapist. They operate the equipment used for heat, sound, and water therapy. Assistants and aides give treatments such as massage and help patients learn and improve physical activities. Physical therapy assistants and aides also keep charts to show how patients are improving.

Physician Assistants

/fih-ZISH-un/ /uh-SIS-tents/

Physician assistants help doctors examine and treat patients. They interview patients and take medical histories. They measure pulse rate, blood pressure, height, and weight for physical exams. Assistants also order laboratory tests and can prescribe medicine for minor illnesses. Many P.A.s work in rural health clinics where there is a shortage of doctors. Others work in emergency services, helping people at the scene of accidents and in the ambulance.

Physicians

/fih-ZISH-uns/

Physicians are doctors who provide what is called primary care to people of all ages. They can diagnose and treat all kinds of infections and illnesses. They deliver babies, stitch cuts, and set broken bones. They refer their patients to medical specialists for specific treatments or surgical procedures.

Physicists

/FIZZ-ih-sists/

Physicists are scientists who study the matter and energy found in the universe. They use mathematical terms to describe the laws and forces of nature. Physicists conduct research on such things as the atom, gravity, lasers, electricity, sound waves, and magnetism. They teach in colleges and universities and also work for industries.

Plasterers

/PLAS-ter-ers/

Plasterers mix and apply plaster materials to walls and ceilings. Plaster is a mixture made from sand, water, and limestone that is treated with chemicals. It does not burn easily and helps to make buildings soundproof. Plasterers use spraying machines or trowels to apply several layers of plaster to walls. Then they smooth the plaster so it can be painted or wallpapered. Plasterers also cover the outside walls of buildings with stucco, a mixture of white cement and sand.

Plastics-Working Machine Operators

/PLAS-tiks-WER-king/ /muh-SHEEN/ /OP-er-ATE-ers/

Like metal products, plastic is molded, cast, and assembled. Workers operate machines which make plastic products. Some machines mix the raw materials or the dyes for colors. Others make the patterns for molds. Liquid plastic is injected into a mold before it hardens. Then workers remove the plastic pieces and assemble all the parts to make things like toys and furniture.

Plumbers and Pipefitters

/PLUM-ers/ and /PIPE-FIT-ters/

Plumbers and pipefitters install and repair pipes that carry water, steam, gas, oil, and sewage. They cut and bend lengths of pipe. They join them together tightly to prevent leaks. Many pipe systems run underground for miles. Plumbers also install sinks and bathroom fixtures and appliances such as dishwashers.

Podiatrists

/po-DY-uh-trists/

Podiatrists diagnose and treat foot problems or diseases. They perform surgery on crooked toes. They may remove corns, bunions, and ingrown toenails. They also prescribe and fit special shoes that can help correct foot problems. Podiatrists teach their patients exercises to improve weak muscles or stiff joints. Many of their patients are athletes and joggers who have foot injuries.

Police, Detectives, and Special Agents

/po-LEECE/ /dee-TEC-tivs/ and /SPEH-shul/ /A-jentz/

Police, detectives, and special agents protect people and property in cities, towns, and rural areas. They make sure that people obey laws and rules of safety. Some police officers direct traffic. Others help prevent crimes, investigate crimes, and arrest people who break the law. Troopers, or highway patrol officers, issue traffic tickets to drivers who disobey laws. They also help at the scene of accidents. Detectives and special agents are plainclothes investigators who gather facts and evidence on criminals. They also participate in raids and arrests.

Political Scientists

/po-**LIT**-ih-kul/ /**SY**-en-tists/

Political scientists study different forms of government. They analyze the ways that national and local laws are made. They are also interested in how countries get along with each other. Some political scientists advise candidates running for office. Others teach in colleges or work for the government.

Printing Press Operators

/**PRINT**-ing/ /press/ /**OP**-er-**ATE**-ers/

Printing press operators run the printing machines, or presses, used to print words and pictures in books, magazines, and newspapers. Operators set up the press by locking in metal plates prepared by desktop publishers and typesetters. They adjust controls on the machines and check the ink and paper flow. Since computers now run many printing presses, some operators work at a control panel and send the right commands through the computer.

Private Household Workers

/**PRY**-vit/ /**HOUSE**-hold/ /**WER**-kers/

Families sometimes hire private household workers to do many jobs in the home. Some workers clean houses. Some cook meals or wash and iron clothes. Others care for lawns and gardens or drive and maintain cars. Some help take care of young children. Maids, butlers, gardeners, chauffeurs, and nannies are all private household workers.

Producers, Directors, and Actors

/pro-**DOOS**-ers/
/dih-**REC**-ters/ and /**AC**-ters/

Producers, directors, and actors may work for television, movies, or live theater. Producers choose scripts for movies, plays, or television. They find people to work on the shows. Producers also need money to pay for everything. Directors study the script, help choose the actors, and guide the work of everyone on the show. Actors learn lines from the script and follow the director's orders.

Proofreaders

/**PROOF**-READ-ers/

Proofreaders carefully read materials that are going to be printed. They check for spelling errors and typing mistakes. They also correct grammar and punctuation errors. Proofreaders work for publishing firms, newspapers, and other printing businesses. Some proofreaders specialize in reading and correcting errors in Braille, a special type of printing for people who are blind.

Property and Real Estate Managers

/**PROP**-er-tee/ and /reel/ /eh-**STATE**/
/**MAN**-uh-jers/

Sometimes owners of shopping centers, apartment buildings, and other properties don't have the time or training to operate them, so they hire property managers. Managers make sure all the spaces are rented, prepare leases, collect the rent, and maintain the property. If owners want to expand, they hire real estate managers to look for any new businesses or properties that might be for sale.

Protestant Ministers

/PRAH-tes-tent/ /MIN-is-ters/

There are many different kinds of churches with many different beliefs. Protestant ministers are the church leaders. Ministers study the beliefs of their church and teach the people who attend. They give sermons and lead worship services. Ministers also conduct weddings and funerals. Some specialize in youth work, education, or music. They counsel people who need help and visit church members who are sick or in the hospital. Some ministers teach at colleges and universities.

Psychologists

/sy-KOL-uh-jists/

Psychologists study and try to understand how human beings learn, think, and get along with each other. They are interested in what makes people behave as they do. Some psychologists conduct research and teach. Others counsel people with problems. Psychologists usually specialize in particular areas of interest such as how children learn, how people choose a career, or what behaviors humans and animals have in common.

Public Relations Specialists

/PUB-lik/ /ree-LAY-shuns/ /SPEH-shul-ists/

Public relations specialists tell people about services or products. They may work for a public relations firm or for a business or other organization. Public relations specialists plan ways to get people's attention in order to tell people the good things a company does. They write articles for magazines, newspapers, television, and radio. They design posters, brochures, and billboards. They also make speeches.

Purchasing Agents and Managers

/PUR-chus-ing/ /A-jentz/ and /MAN-uh-jers/

Purchasing agents and managers order and purchase supplies, materials, and equipment. They work for schools, hospitals, industries, businesses, and government agencies. They order everything from typing paper to office furniture to raw materials used in manufacturing things. Purchasing agents and managers look for the best prices and best quality and also make sure that orders are delivered when promised. Purchasing managers are sometimes called contract managers, procurement officers, or industrial buyers.

Rabbis

/RAB-eyes/

Rabbis are the spiritual leaders of people who share the Jewish heritage and religion. They teach the members of their congregations the history, traditions, laws, and beliefs of the Jewish faith. They lead worship services, deliver sermons, and conduct weddings and funerals. Rabbis also visit the sick and serve as counselors.

Radio and Television Announcers and Newscasters

/RAY-dee-o/ and /TEL-uh-VIH-zhun/ /uh-NOUNCE-ers/ and /NEWS-CAST-ers/

Radio and television announcers and newscasters report news, sports, and weather. They work in broadcasting studios and at the site of special events. Some of them are also disc jockeys who play recorded music and commercials over the radio. Announcers and newscasters often conduct interviews and discuss how current events will affect the nation.

Radiologic Technologists

/RAY-dee-o-LOJ-ik/ /tek-NOL-uh-jists/

Radiologic technologists are also called X-ray technologists. They use X-ray machines, ultrasound, and other equipment to take pictures of the inside of a person's body. This helps doctors diagnose broken bones, cancer, and other problems. Technologists also treat cancer patients with radiation therapy. Most work in hospitals and medical clinics.

Real Estate Agents, Brokers, and Appraisers

/reel/ /eh-STATE/ /A-jentz/ /BRO-kers/ and /uh-PRAY-zers/

Real estate agents and brokers sell land, houses, and buildings. They work with both the sellers and buyers. Real estate workers have to keep track of what is available so they can show it to their clients. Some agents and brokers also rent and manage apartments and offices. Real estate appraisers estimate the value of real estate. They prepare reports for their employers and clients.

Receptionists

/ree-SEP-shun-ists/

Receptionists work near the main entrance or at the front desk of offices and businesses. They are usually the first person a customer or patient sees upon entering. Receptionists greet people and give them directions and other information. Some of them also answer the telephone, make appointments, and perform other clerical duties.

Recreation Workers

/REC-ree-A-shun/ /WER-kers/

Recreation workers plan and organize activities for people of all ages to enjoy in their free time. They work at parks, playgrounds, community centers, camps, and other recreation areas. Some of them direct sports and games, teach people to swim, or lead hikes and nature-study trips. Others teach crafts and hobbies. Some recreation workers specialize in planning activities for the handicapped or for patients in hospitals.

Registered Nurses

/REJ-is-tered/ /NURS-es/

Registered nurses (RNs) care for patients, help doctors, and teach people good health practices. They work in hospitals, doctors' offices, clinics, schools, and in patients' homes. Registered nurses receive special training and must pass a nursing exam before they can practice. Some nurses specialize in one area of medical care, like newborns or the mentally ill.

Reporters and Correspondents

/ree-PORT-ers/ and /COR-uh-SPON-dents/

Reporters and correspondents gather information and write stories about current news events. They collect facts on a topic by doing research, interviewing people, and being present at the scene. Those who work for newspapers and magazines write articles, reviews, and editorials. Television and radio reporters present their stories on camera. All reporters and correspondents work under pressure to meet deadlines.

Reservation and Transportation Ticket Clerks and Travel Clerks

/REZ-er-**VAY**-shun/ and /**TRANS**-por-**TAY**-shun/ /**TIK**-et/ /clerks/ and /**TRAV**-ul/ /clerks/

Reservation agents and transportation ticket clerks help passengers travel from one place to another. They work for airline, railroad, bus, cruise ship, and car-rental companies. Reservation agents give people information about schedules, routes, and the costs of traveling. They reserve seats for people in advance of a trip. Ticket clerks sell tickets, check luggage, and help passengers at boarding stations and terminals. Travel clerks help people plan business trips and vacations by giving information about and arranging for transportation, places to stay, and sightseeing.

Respiratory Therapists

/**RES**-per-uh-**TOR**-ree/ /**THAIR**-uh-pists/

Respiratory therapists help people who have trouble breathing. They work machines to supply oxygen and medication to the lungs. They also teach people how to use breathing machines at home. Therapists also help emergency medical teams who are treating victims of shock, drowning, and heart attacks.

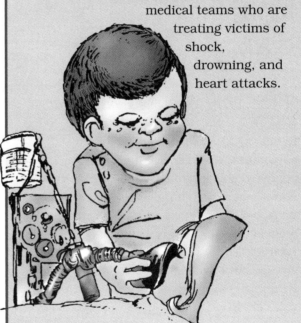

Restaurant and Food Service Managers

/**RES**-ter-ahnt/ and /food/ /**SER**-vis/ /**MAN**-uh-jers/

Restaurant and food service managers work in places where food and drinks are served. Managers supervise all the cooks, servers, cleaners, and cashiers. They plan menus, order food and supplies, and purchase equipment. Managers must also see that workers follow health and safety rules.

Retail Sales Workers

/REE-tail/ /sales/ /WER-kers/

Retail sales workers sell products to customers. They generally work in stores behind the sales counters or "on the sales floor," where merchandise is displayed. Sales workers help people find the correct sizes or models and answer any questions about the product. They also take payments, make change, and wrap or bag purchases. Retail sales workers are sometimes called sales clerks.

Roman Catholic Priests and Nuns

/ROW-man/ /CATH-o-lik/ /preests/ and /nuns/

Roman Catholic priests and nuns are spiritual leaders of people in the Roman Catholic church. Priests lead worship services and perform wedding and funeral ceremonies. Nuns teach, help the sick and the poor, and work in missions all over the world. Nuns and priests serve their God by serving people and teaching people about the Catholic beliefs.

Roofers

/ROOF-ers/

Roofers install roofs on new buildings and replace or repair damaged roofs. They work on flat and slanted roofs, sometimes at great heights. Some roofs are sealed with a hot tar-like material that helps prevent leaks. Others are covered with shingles. Roofers must do a lot of lifting, bending, and climbing and must work outdoors in all types of weather.

Sanitarians

/san-ih-TAIR-ee-uns/

Sanitarians are health and regulatory inspectors who check to make sure that cleanliness and safety rules are followed. They inspect places where food is prepared and served, including dairies, canneries, and restaurants. They also check sewage and garbage disposal systems. Some sanitarians examine water supplies to insure safe drinking water. Others collect air samples to check for pollution.

Sculptors

/SCULP-ters/

Sculptors are artists who shape figures or designs such as statues and monuments. They create forms by carving wood, chiseling marble, modeling clay, and casting or welding metal. Large sculptures are often displayed in museums, parks, gardens, and cemeteries. Sculptors also make small ornamental objects carved with fine details.

Secondary School Teachers

/SEC-un-DAIR-ee/ /skool/ /TEE-chers/

Secondary school teachers teach students in middle schools and high schools. Their college studies prepare them for teaching specific subjects, such as history, science, music, or mathematics. Like all teachers, they plan lessons and assignments, conduct classes, and grade tests and papers. Secondary school teachers also serve as advisors to students and activity clubs. Some also coach sports.

Secretaries

/SEC-ruh-TAIR-ees/

Secretaries work in offices where they do many different things. They type letters and reports. They organize records and files, and run office machines. Secretaries also answer telephones and make appointments. Medical secretaries work with doctors, dentists, and hospitals. They must know medical terms and how to spell them.

Securities and Financial Services Sales Representatives

/seh-KYUR-ih-teez/ and /fy-NAN-chul/ /SER-vis-ses/ /sales/ /REP-pree-ZEN-ta-tivs/

Securities sales representatives help people invest their money. Companies let people buy shares of the business. If the company makes money, the shareholders make a profit. But if the company loses money, so do the shareholders. Representatives, or brokers, have to decide which shares to buy. They must keep up with changes in the economy and new products and businesses. Financial services sales representatives work for banks and other financial organizations. They talk to customers about their banking needs and then tell customers about the banks' services. They can help people open new accounts and request loans.

Security Guards

/seh-KYUR-ih-teel /gards/

Guards protect people, property, and things. They work in many different places. Guards in museums make sure that paintings and exhibits are not stolen or damaged. Guards in banks help prevent thefts. Security guards in office buildings and apartments check the locks on doors and windows. Some guards watch over cars in parking lots. Others check people and cars at entrance gates to special places. Most guards wear uniforms and may carry nightsticks or guns.

Service Station Attendants

/SER-vis/ /STAY-shun/ /uh-TEN-dants/

At most service stations, customers fill their own cars with gas. Service station attendants work inside collecting money, making change, and selling snack foods and other small items, like maps, sunglasses, or window washing fluid. They also keep the service station areas neat and clean. Some stations have a "full service" area and attendants pump gas, check the oil and other fluids, and check the tires, belts, and other engine parts. Some work with mechanics and help with repairs.

Services Sales Representatives

/SER-vis-ses/ /sales/
/REP-pree-ZEN-ta-tivs/

Some companies sell services. Customers need cable, telephone service, laundry service, lawn maintenance, and garbage collection. Sales representatives explain the service and its cost. They answer any questions, write up contracts, and make sure the customer is happy with the results. They also take care of any customer problems.

Set and Exhibit Designers

/set/ and /ex-IB-it/
/dee-ZINE-ers/

Set designers create the "sets"—all of the rooms on the stage where movies and television programs are made. They have to study scripts and talk to the show's director to learn what the story is about. They might have to read about clothing and furniture from long ago to make the set look the way it should. They make sketches or small models to show what the full-sized set should look like. Then they build the actual full-sized set. Exhibit designers work with museums, art galleries, and convention halls that are using their buildings to put on everything from art shows to car shows. The exhibit designer looks at the space that they want to use and

decides where lights should go, where each piece of art should be hung or each car should be parked, and how the space can be used the best.

Sheet Metal Workers

/sheet/ /MET-ul/ /WER-kers/

Sheet metal workers construct products made from thin, flat pieces of metal. These products include such things as ducts for furnaces and stoves, tin roofs, aluminum siding, and rain gutters. Sheet metal workers follow blueprints and patterns to cut and shape the metal. They bolt, weld, rivet, or solder (sod-der) the pieces together.

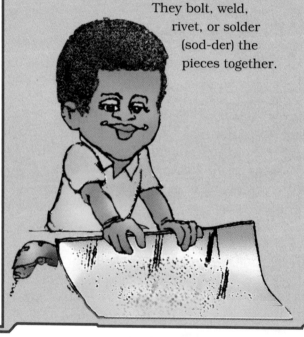

Shoe and Leather Workers and Repairers

/shoo/ and /LETH-er/ /WER-kers/ and /re-PAIR-ers/

Shoe repairers mend shoes, handbags, belts, suitcases, and other leather goods. They use special machines and tools to cut and stitch leather. They also replace worn soles and heels so that shoes will last longer. Some shoe repairers have their own shops and sell shoes, laces, polish, and other leather goods. Factory leather workers tan and finish skins to produce leather products such as clothing, shoes, furniture, and purses. Shoe industry workers produce shoes made on more than 300 different machines. Other workers cut hides; prepare insoles, outsoles, and heels; assemble shoes; and finish products.

Social Workers

/SO-shul/ /WER-kers/

Social workers help people lead healthier, happier lives. Some people need counseling, financial support, or some kind of information. Social workers decide what kind of help people need and make sure they get it. They work with government and community programs that help people who are poor, hungry, homeless, or unable to work. They also help troubled families, hospital patients, prisoners, and those who are old.

Sociologists

/SO-see-OL-uh-jists/

People live and work in groups like families, tribes, communities, governments, churches, and gangs. Sociologists study people and the groups they form. They are interested in how people behave in groups and get along with each other. They hope that this information will help us understand social problems like crime or prejudice.

Speech/Language Pathologists and Audiologists

/speech/ /LANG-gwij/
/puh-THOL-uh-jists/
and /AW-dee-OL-uh-jists

Speech/language pathologists and audiologists work with adults and children who have speaking and hearing problems. These medical specialists find out what causes the problem and decide the best treatment. Sometimes treatment can include a hearing aid or surgery. Special exercises for the tongue and mouth and practicing certain sounds can help people learn to speak correctly. Audiologists are also called hearing specialists.

Statisticians

/STAT-is-TISH-uns/

Statisticians use a special kind of math called statistics to describe and to predict things. They do research and collect information about people and natural science. Then they use numbers to measure and compare. Statisticians might figure out how fast the population of a city will grow or how many people will probably live to be 100 years old. They work for businesses and the government.

Stock Clerks

/stok/ /clerks/

Stock clerks are responsible for ordering and organizing extra supplies and products for stores, businesses, or hospitals. They keep careful records called inventories. They count the merchandise, foods, medicines, or machinery parts in the stockroom. In a store, stock clerks keep shelves, racks, and counters stocked with products for customers. In a hospital, stock clerks are responsible for keeping extra supplies of bandages, medicines, towels, or instruments.

Subway and Street Car Operators

/SUB-WAY/ and /street/ /car/ /OP-er-ATE-ers/

Operators drive the cars, collect fares, and must obey traffic signals. They control trains which usually run in tunnels underground. They watch for signals on the tracks that tell them when to stop and start the train. They make announcements, open and close the doors, and look for any problems. Street car operators run electric-powered cars. These cars move on the street like automobiles.

Surgeons

/SER-jens/

There are many kinds of doctors. Surgeons operate on patients to repair injuries, prevent diseases, or improve health. Operations usually involve organs, bones, or tissues inside the body. Surgeons use special instruments to cut and sew. They work in hospitals where nurses and others help them. They need excellent hand-eye coordination.

Surgical Technologists

/SER-ji-kul/ /tek-NOL-uh-jists/

These workers help patients and surgeons during surgery. They set up the operating room and make sure everything is very clean or sterile. Another job is getting patients ready for surgery. Germs can make people sick, so technologists make sure the patient's skin is clean before the doctor begins. During surgery, they pass instruments and supplies to the doctors. Sometimes tissue samples need to be tested, so technologists take them to the laboratory.

Surveyors

/ser-VAY-ers/

Surveyors make precise measurements and decide the boundaries of areas of land or water. They use special instruments, draw maps, and write descriptions of the places they measure. These are used when highways, pipelines, bridges, and houses are built. Surveyors work outdoors. They must pass a test given by the state to get a license to work.

Taxi Drivers and Chauffeurs

/TAX-ee/ /DRY-vers/ and /SHOW-fers/

Taxi drivers and chauffeurs drive passengers from one place to another in towns and cities. Taxis are usually equipped with meters that register the fare based on the distance traveled. Some drivers own their own taxi cabs. Others work for companies that own many cabs. Taxi drivers work day and night. They must know the streets and areas of a city very well. Chauffeurs drive private cars, limousines, and hearses for owners or other passengers. They assist passengers in and out of cars. They also keep vehicles clean and in operating condition.

Teacher Aides

/TEE-cher/ /aids/

Teacher aides help teachers with many of their school duties so that teachers will have more time to teach their students. Aides help in the classroom, the library, the cafeteria, and on the playground. They record grades, check homework, duplicate work sheets, and supervise study time. They collect lunch money and check attendance. Many teacher aides also work with individual students or small groups.

Technical Writers

/TEK-nih-kul/ /RYE-ters/

Technical writers communicate information about science and technology. They help scientists, doctors, and others write scientific and medical reports. They take information and make it easy for everyone to understand. Writers must explain things clearly since most people do not know technical terms. They also write computer manuals, catalogs, and the instructions that tell how to use and repair a product.

Telephone Line Installers and Repairers

/TEL-uh-fone/ /line/ /in-STALL-ers/ and /re-PAIR-ers/

Telephone line installers and repairers are technicians. They work with telephones, switchboard systems, and the equipment for radio and television broadcasts. These technicians travel to customers' homes and offices to install and repair equipment. They must follow the instructions in technical manuals and diagrams of circuit wiring. They also climb telephone poles and towers or use trucks with cranes to work on overhead wires and cables.

Tilesetters

/**TILE**-SET-ers/

Tilesetters apply ceramic or acoustical tiles to floors, walls, and ceilings. They cut the tiles to fit exactly in corners or around tubs, sinks, and faucets. Then they use trowels to spread cement paste on the surface they are covering. After they set the tiles in place, they fill the spaces between tiles with grout, a very fine cement. Tilesetters must bend, stretch, reach, climb ladders, and measure skillfully.

Timber Cutting and Logging Workers

/**TIM**-ber/ /**CUT**-ting/ and /**LOG**-ing/ /**WER**-kers/

Felling trees and cutting them into logs is just one of the jobs in the logging industry. Cruisers identify trees ready for harvest. Fallers cut down trees with axes and chainsaws. Buckers cut limbs and trunks into pieces. Many other types of workers help transport the logs to sawmills. There, workers cut, edge, trim, plane, dry, and grade lumber. They also maintain the mill's equipment.

Tool and Diemakers

/tool/ and /**DIE**-MAKE-ers/

Tool and diemakers produce metal tools and the equipment used to form metal parts for industrial machinery. They make jigs and fixtures, which hold metal while it is bored, drilled, and stamped. Diemakers also construct molds (dies) into which hot metal or plastic is poured for shaping. These workers must be skilled in working with cutting, shaping, and measuring tools.

Tool Programmers, Numerical Control

/tool/ /PRO-gram-ers/ /new-MAIR-ih-kul/ /con-TROL/

Some tool-making machines are run by computers. These machines manufacture metal parts for planes, cars, and industrial machinery. Tool programmers study blueprints and decide how to make the part. They need to know about metals such as cast iron, steel, and aluminum. Then, tool programmers write programs in code to operate the machines. Built-in computers read the instructions and the machine does the work.

Traffic, Shipping, and Receiving Clerks

/TRAF-fic/ /SHIP-ing/ and /ree-SEE-ving/ /clerks/

Traffic, shipping, and receiving clerks help move products from one place to another. Traffic clerks fill the orders and send products from factories to stores and from stores to customers. Shipping clerks wrap and weigh packages and containers. They figure out the cost of postage and freight. They may help load products on trucks, trains, ships, and planes. Receiving clerks check to be sure orders have been filled correctly and that nothing has been lost or damaged. These clerks usually work in company warehouses and stockrooms.

Travel Agents

/TRAV-ul/ /A-jentz/

Travel agents help people make plans for vacations and business trips. They make arrangements in advance for transportation, hotel reservations, and even sightseeing trips. They also provide information about prices and fares, passports, and the money systems of foreign countries.

Truckdrivers

/TRUCK-DRY-vers/

Truckdrivers move many different things from one place to another. Some drive local delivery trucks and vans. Others drive trucks for construction firms, gas companies, wrecker services, or lumberyards. Long-distance truckdrivers haul big tractor-trailer rigs or car carriers across the country. Truckdrivers need a special driver's license and a good driving record.

Underwriters

/UN-der-RYE-ters/

Underwriters work for insurance companies. They check on applications for life, health, or property coverage. They decide whether or not to sell insurance to a person or a business. Sometimes an underwriter might find out that a driver has caused several traffic accidents or has gotten too many speeding tickets. The underwriter may decide that insuring that person would be a risk.

Upholsterers

/uh-POLE-ster-ers/

Upholsterers make furniture last longer and can make chairs and sofas look new again. They cover them with new fabric. They also replace worn springs and old padding, make new cushions, and re-glue loose sections of the wood frame and legs. Some upholsterers specialize in reconditioning automobile seats. Upholsterers use tools for cutting, heavy-duty sewing machines, and hammers and tacks.

Urban and Regional Planners

/UR-bun/ and /REE-jun-ul/
/PLAN-ners/

Urban and regional planners help cities and communities plan for the future. They study how land is used and how the population of an area is growing. Then they consider the need for new housing, utilities, roads, transportation systems, and services. They recommend the best locations for new hospitals, shopping centers, and industries. Most planners work for local, state, and federal governments.

Vehicle Washers and Equipment Cleaners

/VEE-ih-kul/ /WASH-ers/
and /ee-KWIP-ment/
/CLEEN-ers/

Washers and cleaners are found everywhere. Businesses need to keep equipment clean and working well. Every city has car washes. Many of these jobs are good for beginners because workers don't need any experience. Some jobs are hard and include lifting, kneeling, and crawling. Washers and cleaners must follow directions and may work either inside or outside.

Vending Machine Servicers and Repairers

/VEN-ding/ /muh-SHEEN/ /SER-vis-ers/
and /re-PAIR-ers/

Vending machine servicers and repairers work on coin-operated machines. These machines include candy and soft drink machines, laundromat appliances, and video games. These workers keep the electrical and refrigeration systems and change mechanisms in good working order. They must also keep the machines stocked with coins and merchandise.

Veterinarians

/VET-er-ih-**NAIR**-ee-uns/

Veterinarians are doctors who treat both large and small animals. They care for pets, farm animals, and animals in zoos or on wildlife preserves. Veterinarians also do important work for people's health. They investigate disease outbreaks and conduct research to test new medicines.

Veterinary Assistants and Nonfarm Animal Caretakers

/**VET**-er-uh-NAIR-ee/
/uh-**SIS**-tents/
and /non-farm/
/**AN**-ih-mul/
/**CARE**-take-ers/

Veterinary assistants help the veterinarian take care of animals and birds. They feed and water them according to a schedule. They may also sterilize equipment and instruments used by the veterinarian. Animal caretakers also take care of animals. They may clean and disinfect cages, pens, and yards. Sometimes they shave, bathe, clip, and groom animals. Caretakers may be asked to repair cages, pens, or fenced yards. Assistants and caretakers work in places such as kennels, animal shelters, pet stores, stables, and zoos.

Waiters and Waitresses

/**WAY**-ters/
and /**WAY**-tress-es/

Waiters and waitresses may also be called waitpersons. They provide service to customers in restaurants. They take the customers' orders to the cooks, serve food and beverages, and make out the bill or "check". Sometimes they also take payments and operate the cash register. Waiters and waitresses are expected to provide courteous, efficient service.

Water and Wastewater Treatment Plant Operators

/WAH-ter/ and /WAYST-WAH-ter/ /TREET-ment/ /plant/ /OP-er-ATE-ers/

Water and wastewater treatment plant operators manage the systems that provide water and sewage disposal for towns and cities. They chemically test and treat water so that it is safe to drink. They also keep meters, pumps, valves, and pipes in good working order. These workers are especially concerned about controlling water pollution.

Water Transportation Workers

/WAH-ter/ /TRANS-por-TAY-shun/ /WER-kers/

Many jobs exist on large cargo ships, troop carriers, tankers, ferries, and cruise ships. These ships transport goods and passengers across the seas. Captains navigate the ships and are in charge of the crew. Mates have certain duties like using navigation charts and equipment and maintaining lifeboats and firefighting gear. Engineers operate the huge engines and maintain and repair the machinery. Stewards are in charge of supplies, living quarters, and meals on board.

Welders, Cutters, and Welding Machine Operators

/WEL-ders/ /CUT-ters/ and /WEL-ding/ /muh-SHEEN/ /OP-er-ATE-ers/

Welders and welding machine operators trim and join pieces of metal by using heat to melt and fuse the metal. Welding torches and machines create heat with electricity or gas. Skillful welders know the melting points of steel, aluminum, and other metals. They weld steel beams, iron pipes, and large metal plates for building ships and planes. Welding machine operators set up and operate welding machines which have automatic controls. Cutters use burning gases or an electric arc to cut and trim metal. Welders, cutters, and welding machine operators wear special clothes and helmets for protection from burns and possible injuries.

Woodworkers

/WOOD-WER-kers/

Woodworkers have a variety of jobs and each requires special skills. Carpenters build buildings. But finish carpenters, trimmers, and cabinetmakers do the detailed work. Furniture manufacturers hire workers to cut, shape, and assemble wood. Patternmakers carve molds out of wood. Some woodworkers create custom pieces of furniture, bowls, sculptures, and other carvings.

Writers and Editors

/RYE-ters/ and /ED-it-ers/

People read for information and for pleasure. Writers and editors provide the reading material. Writers put ideas, feelings, and observations into interesting words and sentences. They write fiction, poetry, scientific reports, newspaper and magazine articles, biographies, and even school textbooks. Editors check the work of writers. Sometimes editors suggest changes or new ideas. Editors make sure that the writer's work is ready for printing and publishing.

Word Processors, Typists, and Data Entry Workers

/word/ /PRAH-SES-sers/ /TYP-ists/ and /DAY-tuh/ /EN-tree/ /WER-kers/

Word processors, typists, and data entry workers help businesses process and organize information. Word processors use computers to create, edit, store, and change letters, reports, and other printed material. Typists usually take materials written by others and make neat, accurate, printed copies. Data entry keyers enter numbers and type data from documents. Workers must communicate well and should be able to read, write, spell, and proofread. They should also be able to work fast with their hands and fingers. Many people start their careers as typists or data entry workers and then move to other jobs.

Getting a Job

Perhaps you've already had some work for which you earned money. These may be chores around the house or yard or helping a neighbor care for plants or a pet. But what about when you're older and you want to get a part-time job after school or in the summer? What do you do? By the time you are 16, you are likely to be seeking a part-time job.

Most communities have rules about how old you have to be to be employed. And, employers have rules about how many hours you can work, and how late you can work. You will need to know these things before you begin a search for a job.

Sometime teenagers volunteer for work with no pay. As a volunteer you get experience doing things that may lead to a job. Another way to get experience is to be an intern. Some employers have internships. An internship allows a person to learn about work that may be of interest. An intern may or may not be paid for the work.

Do I Want a Job or a Career?

Is there a difference between a job and a career?

A job is any work that people do for money. Some jobs may be done for experience. Jobs may use an individual's talents, abilities, or skills and then again . . . some may not. Some people may not even like their jobs. There are many reasons why people do work they don't enjoy:
* They may not have the right skills or education to get a job they want
* There is a lot of competition for certain jobs
* They may have lost a job they liked and can't find another

A career is a series or group of related jobs. The jobs share common interests, knowledge, training and experience. For example: Jenna wanted to be a chef. In high school, she worked at a fast-food restaurant washing dishes. This was a job. As time went by, Jenna worked her way up to short-order cook. She also worked in many different restaurants. As she gained experience, she got closer to her goal. Finally, a major restaurant hired Jenna as a chef. She is now thinking about writing a cookbook.

Jenna's career choice was to become a chef. She worked at many different, but related, jobs to reach her goal. This is called a career path. The jobs may be very similar, like in the food service work, or very different. The key in choosing a career path is to find things that interest you and that use your special abilities.

Below is a diagram of another kind of career path. In this example, the person went from teaching ... to banking ... to marketing and advertising ... to editing ... and finally to television announcer. Even though each job was very different, they all had certain things in common. These "common things" are what make a career path. You can find job titles that deal with these areas in the Dictionary.

As you look at the Children's Dictionary, you may find interesting jobs. Some you may not like. Try to decide what makes a job sound interesting and what doesn't. You need to know about your own likes or dislikes and skills and abilities. It will make it easier to make choices about your future when you begin to find your own career path.

How Do I Find a Job?

The first thing you have to do is find a job. You have used the Children's Dictionary and may have noticed that some jobs need a lot of education or experience while others don't. Since most teens don't have work experience, it's probably best to look for work that doesn't require it. This type of work is called entry-level. Employers don't mind hiring workers and training them. Some examples of entry-level jobs are fast-food workers, clerical workers, amusement or recreation workers, and laborers.

What Is a Résumé? (REZ-uh-may)

This French word means a short account of a person's abilities. You write out all of the things that you are qualified to do. It's important to list all of the jobs you have had. A résumé gives the dates of the jobs. If you haven't had many or any jobs, you can talk about your skills and accomplishments. These might be speaking a foreign language or typing or knowing how to use a computer. You may want to list any classes you've taken that would be helpful on the job.

Employers are also interested in any volunteer or extra-curricular activities (like sports, decorating for dances, being in plays, or maybe tutoring younger students).

The next two pages show two sample résumés (Figures 1 and 2). The first one shows work experience and education. The second one shows skills and accomplishments.

Do I Have to Send a Cover Letter?

Whenever you send a résumé to an employer, you should write a letter to go with it. It explains who you are and why you're sending a résumé. Although you can send copies of your résumé, each cover letter must be written individually. It's a good idea to find out who is to receive the letter and use that person's name in the letter. Make sure there are no spelling or typing errors. Anyone reading this letter will form a first impression about who wrote it, so neatness counts. Check out the example shown in Figure 3.

Figure 1. Chronological Résumé (information listed by dates)

1 Angela Fish
6461 Arrowhead Street
Webster Groves, MO 63199
314-555-8210

2 JOB OBJECTIVE
Seeking a position as a receptionist. Desire position with opportunity for career growth.

3 WORK EXPERIENCE

September 2003 - present	Sales Associate, Bright Clothes Emporium, Webster Groves, Missouri. Responsible for customer service, some record keeping, and inventory.
August 2002 - May 2003	Counter attendant, Happy Jack's Burgers & More, Webster Groves, Missouri. Took and filled customer orders. Promoted to assistant manager within 4 months.
Summers. 2001 and 2002	Swimming instructor, Anna High School, Webster Groves, Missouri. Taught diving and life-saving techniques to intermediate level students.

4 EDUCATION
Graduated June 2004 from Anna High School, Webster Groves, Missouri, with a grade point average of 3.2 on a 4.0 scale.

5 HONORS AND ACTIVITIES
Dean's Honor List, Student Council Member, Yearbook Sports Editor, Swimming Team Member

6 SPECIAL SKILLS AND ABILITIES
Keyboarding and word processing. Use both Macintosh and IBM-compatible computers. Strong math skills. Excellent attendance record.

7 REFERENCES
Available upon request.

---

1. Name and Address. At the top of your résumé, put your full name, address, and phone number.
2. Job Objective: State the job you want. If you are too specific, you might not be considered for anything else. If you are too vague, the employer might not be interested.
3. Work Experience: List all of your jobs, beginning with the most recent, and list dates.
4. Education: List the schools you have attended and diplomas or degrees you have earned.
5. Honors and Activities: Note any activities or honors, especially if they relate to the job you want.
6. Special Skills and Abilities: List any skills you have gained whether in school or elsewhere and any special abilities you possess.
7. References: Always ask permission to use people as references. You may list them if you have enough room—but make sure your résumé is easy to read and not too crowded.

Figure 2. Skills Résumé

1 Robert Brown
2025 N. Lyon St.
Kirkwood, MO 63122
314/555-7734

2 JOB OBJECTIVE
Seeking a position as an editor's assistant.

3 SKILLS AND ABILITIES
Computer Skills: Comfortable working with IBM-compatible computers. Scored in top 10% of computer classes in middle and high school.

Communications: Excellent writing and speaking skills. Good with grammar and usage. Received A's in all English and speech classes and have had short stories published in the high school journal.

Hardworking: Am responsible for all yardwork at home, including mowing, weeding, and trimming. Have also worked as a swimming instructor during summer vacation.

Customer Relations: Work well with people. The swimming classes I taught increased during every session and my supervisor told me the students liked my teaching style. I was asked back the following summer.

Attention to Detail: I am precise and careful in my work. I was the student editor for the school newspaper as a sophomore and was responsible for proofreading and making corrections. My faculty sponsor said I was one of the best editors she had ever worked with.

4 ACTIVITIES AND AWARDS
Student council member, school newspaper student editor, member of the swimming team, and Dean's honor list every semester since 6th grade.

1. Name and Address. At the top of your résumé, put your full name, address, and phone number.
2. Job Objective: State the job you want. If you are too specific, you might not be considered for anything else. If you are too vague, the employer might not be interested.
3. Special Skills and Abilities: List any skills you have gained, whether in school or elsewhere, and any special abilities you possess. You are describing in detail those strengths that will make you a good person for the job. This can be very valuable if you don't have a work history.
4. Activities and Awards: Note any activities or awards, especially if they relate to the job you want. This section helps an employer get an idea of what kind of person you are. The kinds of activities you do may also show that you can take on responsibility.

Figure 3. Cover Letter

June 1, 2004

Bob Smith
Acme Publishing Company
236 E. Front Street
Bloomington, IL 61701

Dear Mr. Smith:

Barbara Lang, Co-op director at Winston High School, suggested that I contact you about the position for junior production editor. I would like to apply for this position.

I will be a senior next year at Winston High School and will be participating in the co-op program. For the last three years, I worked on the Winston Wiretap, our weekly school newspaper, and eventually became the editor this last year. I learned paste-up, proofing, editing, and some desktop publishing during this time. I was responsible for meeting deadlines and can say that the paper was never late while I was editor.

I have included a résumé which provides some more details about the skills I can offer for this position. I would be available all day during the summer and from 12:00 noon until closing time during the school year.

I am hoping to pursue a career in editing and believe that a co-op internship with your publishing company would be a wonderful experience before I go to college and after. I also believe that my enthusiasm and eagerness to learn would be beneficial to you.

May I schedule an interview? My home phone number is 309-555-2713.

Sincerely,

Lauren Collier
2739 Briar Lane
Bloomington, IL 61701

Why Do I Need an Application?

When you apply for a job, you will most likely fill out an application form. Employers use application forms to get information about you. An application gives skills, experience, and other things. Keep the following tips in mind:

* Read and follow all of the instructions exactly.
* Print neatly so your answers can be easily read.
* Don't scratch out answers and write over. If you make a mistake and cannot erase, ask for another application form.

* Write out a list of information you may need and take it with you:
  - schools attended and dates
  - personal references—including addresses and phone numbers
  - previous jobs—including dates you started and ended
* Don't ever lie on an application. If you think a truthful answer may disqualify you, write "will explain in interview."

Please look at the sample application in Figure 4.

Figure 4. Job Application

JOB APPLICATION FORM

Date of application _____

Full name: _____
            first   middle initial   last

Address: _____

City _____ State _____ Zip _____

Home telephone (_____) _____

Position applied for _____

When will you be available for work? _____

Please complete the following information:

EDUCATION

	School name & address	Number of years attended	Did you graduate?	Major or degree
High School				
College				
Trade School or other				
Special training				

_____

EMPLOYMENT HISTORY (start with most recent work)

Name and address of employer	Dates employed (from month/year to month/year)	Kind of work	Reason for leaving

REFERENCES

Name/ Relationship	Full address	Telephone

SPECIAL SKILLS (foreign languages, computer)

_____

_____

Are Interviews Important?

Someone wants to talk to you about a job! What do you do—or better yet—what don't you do?

It's important to make a good impression on the interviewer by the way you look, the way you act, and what you say.

Appearance:
* Dress appropriately
    - wear clothing that is suitable for the job and if you're unsure, ask someone
    - no dirty, torn jeans and sweatshirts, or ball caps
    - no tight, revealing clothing
    - no wild jewelry, extravagant hair styles, or bright nail polish
* Be neat and clean
    - no heavy make-up
    - no perfume/cologne and easy on the hair spray
* Shine your shoes—little things matter

Behavior:
* Be on time and come alone
* Shake hands with the interviewer and look him/her in the eyes
* Don't sit until you're invited to do so
* Sit up straight and pay attention
* Never chew gum

Conversation
* Think about why you want this job and practice saying it out loud
* Listen carefully to each question and answer clearly
    - don't give one-word answers like yes and no
    - explain your answers in complete sentences, using standard English
    - don't mumble—speak loud enough to be heard
    - if you don't understand a question, say so
* Keep good eye contact with the other person while you're speaking
* Be prepared to ask some questions about the company
* Have a positive attitude and be enthusiastic
* Shake hands with the interviewer when you leave and thank him or her
* Write a thank-you note to the interviewer and mail it the next day

What Are Work Skills?

You got the job! Your résumé was outstanding ... your interview was wonderful ... and you start tomorrow. First, you'll be asked to fill out some forms. Most of these forms are for withholding taxes. Next, your employer will probably show you around and introduce you to your co-workers. Then the training begins. Learning new things can be scary, but no matter what the job, there are certain basic things that every employee needs to know:

1. Always arrive on time for work.
   - if you have to be absent or late, call your supervisor as soon as possible
   - too many absences might tell an employer that you are not reliable

2. Be prepared.
   - have whatever you need and be ready to go on time
   - if you wear a uniform, make sure it is clean and pressed

3. Ask questions and make sure you understand what you are to do.

4. Follow the company rules.

5. Always be polite and respectful.

6. Get along with your co-workers.

7. Accept criticism politely.
   - everyone makes mistakes, especially in a new job
   - listening to criticism with a positive attitude will help you learn
   - no one likes to work with people who complain or become angry

Job Titles in Occupational Clusters

Agriculture, Food & Natural Resources

Architecture & Construction

Arts, A/V Technology & Communications

Hospitality & Tourism

Human Services

Information Technology

Law, Public Safety & Security

Manufacturing

Marketing, Sales & Service

Science, Technology, Engineering & Mathematics

Transportation, Distribution & Logistics

Alphabetical Index